I0560411

ISBN 979-8-9993516-4-7

Edited and Formatted by Represent Publishing

Cover Designs by Brittany Evans @ BEDESIGNS.CA

MIND-BODY CONNECTION

Unlocked

MIND-BODY
CONNECTION
Unlocked

MARY ELAINE CLAVIERES

Represent
Publishing

May this assist you in your greatest expansion.
- Fuana

To Evie and Elena,
May you live your life with full embodiment and the highest expression of who you came here to be. Thank you for choosing me.

To Remy,
The love of my life, thank you for being you. Thank you for your endless encouragement. Your unwavering faith in me was my guiding light in making this book become a reality.

CONTENTS

Author's Note   xv
Introduction   xix
How To Use This Book   xxi

PART 1: UNDERSTANDING THE MIND-BODY CONNECTION

Introduction   3
The Science of the Mind-Body Connection   5
Reflection 1.1: Mind-Body Connection   13
Healing Modalities   16
My Experience with the Mind-Body Connection   21
Part 1: Key Takeaways   22

PART 2: THE WHOLE SELF

My Story   27
Understanding the Whole Self   31
Embracing Self-Responsbility   34
Reflection 2.1: Self-Awareness   38
Taking Care of Your Whole Self   41
5 Pillars of Self-Care   47
Addressing Blocks to Living as Your Whole Self   55
Reflection: 2.2: Fears   59
Coming Back to Your Whole Self When You
Feel Lost   63
Activity: 2.1: Creative Outlets   65
Reflection 2.3: Self-Expression   67
Part 2: Key Takeaways   69
Additional Activities & Tools for the Whole Self   73
Activity 2.2: Self Check Ins   74
Activity 2.3: Setting Intentions   76
Activity 2.4: Identify Your Values   83
Tool 2.1: Journaling   86
Tool 2.2: Walks in Nature   88
Tool 2.3: Meditation   90

PART 3: THE MIND

Understanding the Mind   97
What Holds You Back   99
Activity 3.1: Identify Your Fears   101
Mental Blocks   104
The Truth Is . . .   108
Activity 3.2: The Truth Is . . .   110
Creating a New Reality   112
Activity 3.3: Build Your Gratitude Practice   124
Part 3: Key Takeaways   126
Additional Activities & Tools for the Mind   129
Activity 3.4: Transform Your Thoughts   130
Activity 3.5: Reframe Your Mistakes   133
Tool 3.1: Affirmations   135

PART 4: THE BODY

Understanding the Body   141
The Mind-Body Relationship   144
The Physical Body   146
Activity 4.1: Speak to Your Body   149
The Energy Body   151
The Emotional Body   155
Activity 4.2: Get Into Your Body   161
A New Way of Being   162
Part 4: Key Takeaways   167
Additional Activities & Tools for the Body   169
Activity 4.3: Pay Attention To Your Body   170
Activity 4.4: Self-Care For Your Body   172
Tool 4.1: Tapping   173
Tool 4.2: Body Scan   177

PART 5: THE SOUL

Understanding the Soul   185
Navigating Your Soul Expansion   188
Blocks to Your Soul   191
Recognizing Recurring Patterns in Your Life   193
Activity 5.1: Identifying Patterns   198
The Continued Depths of Gratitude   201
The Power of Prayer   205
Activity 5.2: Sample Prayer   207

Seeing Synchronicity   209
Part 5: Key Takeaways   211
Additional Activities & Tools for the Soul   213
Activity 5.3: Your Soul's Calling   214
Activity 5.4: Re-Write Your Soul Story   217
Tool 5.1: Working With The Four Elements   221
Tool 5.2: Breathing Through Your Entire Body   224

PART 6: INTEGRATION

Living Your Mind-Body Soul Aligned Life   231
Making Daily Aligned Choices   232
Building Emotional Resilience & Consistency   234
Planning Your Day—Finding What Works for You   239
Overcoming Obstacles   243
Moving About the World Differently   250
Part 6: Key Takeaways   252

Conclusion   255

Resources   259
Thank You!   261
Acknowledgments   263
About The Author   267
Notes   269
Bibliography   275

Author's Note

I've always been a seeker. Of what exactly, I wasn't sure. But I always knew there was something out there for me. Something bigger than me, grander than me, and certainly more powerful than me. Looking back, I realize the same things that I was seeking were seeking me. The thing is, none of it was outside of me—it was all within.

Through my experience discovering the mind-body connection, I learned your soul is the true driver of your life. Most of the time, we let the mind decide yes or no to our opportunities and choices. We shut down our bodies and ignore our pain until we can't take it anymore and are forced to address it (burnout, for example).

The soul is *meant* to be in the driver's seat. It nudges you to choose one path, or not choose another—*if you listen to it*. At the heart of it, the soul wants to guide you through the intuitive reflexes of your body and use the education of the mind as a support system. All working together in harmony for your highest alignment.

As you awaken your mind-body connection, you'll start to

feel the depths of your soul in ways you haven't experienced before. I cannot truly describe the depth of beauty and exquisiteness that is this experience. My hope is that by reading this book and exploring the tools and activities to awaken your mind-body connection, you will have this experience for yourself.

The journey of life is like an onion. You peel back a layer at a time. Sometimes you hit a snag or a rough patch, but you keep going. You keep making your way to the center. I personally don't believe you ever actually arrive at the center, but you get closer and closer by peeling back more layers. When you continue to learn, grow, try new things, get curious about your life, and really look within you, it takes you closer to your divine self. This is the process of you discovering the you that you came here to be.

No one else could walk my journey for me. My expansion rested in every step and invitation—to choose strength instead of shrinking, compassion instead of anger, and trust instead of fear. It continues to this day and will continue as long as I am alive in this form.

This journey is not for everyone, but since you are reading this book, you likely already feel a higher calling. If you don't understand it or can't make sense of it in this moment, that is ok. This book will support you in peeling back your own layers in your own way.

As you activate your mind-body connection, the more connected you will be to this planet and all it has to offer. What a beautiful gift to receive in this lifetime.

Unconditionally,
Mary Clavieres
May 2025

Personal Growth Mantra:

I am aligned to my highest potential and open
to the infinite possibilities within the universe
that are available to me.

Introduction

Welcome to *Mind-Body Connection Unlocked: Simple Mind-Body Techniques to Rewire Your Mind, Deepen Your Self-Connection, and Gently Transform the Way You Live.*

This book is here to support you on your personal transformation journey. It's here to show you that you can trust yourself more than anyone else in the world and you'll be divinely supported when doing so.

We live in a busy world with a lot of noise. The practical tools and exercises shared in this book will show you ways to quiet your mind in order to connect with your body and the essence of who you truly are. It is supportive to busy schedules with some of the exercises only taking 1-3 minutes. Quality over quantity is a sentiment infused into this book because I truly believe that small steps can have a big impact. The goal is for you to live a life that incorporates the whole of who YOU are, not who others have told you to be.

Our culture doesn't necessarily support the belief that everyone has this within themselves, but they do. By learning about the interconnectedness of your mind, body, and soul (also known as spirit or higher self) and integrating these parts of you to work together, you will unlock new doors to truly change your life.

This book is for you if you are searching for more in your life. You may feel lost, broken, stuck, or unsure of where to go next. You may feel curious and energized by the possibilities of what lies before you. Wherever you are is ok.

I believe life is too short to just go through the motions. It's too short to be wishing for weekends or retirement. While everyone is not in the same place in terms of privilege or equity, my hope is that the tools and resources in this book can support you, wherever it finds you in this moment.

The intention of this book is to build a bridge. It's meant to help you connect to the possibilities you see for your future— whatever they may look like for you. Whether you consider yourself a very practical person or a more spiritual one, this book is connecting worlds to show you what is meant for you is beyond your wildest dreams—if you allow it.

It's important to me that you receive many different tools you can experiment with and incorporate into your life. Life is not a one size fits all and neither is this book. Take what resonates and leave the rest behind. This book will include both scientific modalities (i.e. cognitive behavioral therapy) and natural modalities (i.e. somatic therapy) along with an overall holistic approach to life.

Remember, life is not a competition or a race. There is no arrival point. It is an experience of living in every moment.

When you ask people that are on their deathbed about their regrets, they do not regret how much more they could have worked on achieving a certain status. Their number one regret is: "I wish I'd had the courage to live a life true to myself, not the life others expected of me."[1]

My hope is by the end of this book, you can live your life with deeper meaning and more alignment to achieve your dreams, without the weight of others' expectations.

How To Use This Book

This book is divided into six parts. It is best to first read this book from cover to cover to discover the full mind-body connection process. Then, you can go back to specific parts you were drawn to. Activities and reflection questions are spread throughout the book to support you on your journey. Tools are also included as a way to build your personal toolbox. Anytime you need to work through something or self-regulate, choose what calls to you in that moment. We are all unique and I honor where you are in your life and your process. Trust that what you choose will support your highest alignment.

Check in with yourself to see where you need the most support in this moment. Trust what you feel and start from there. As you continue to grow and evolve, you can choose another section to support your next area of focus.

A few things to keep in mind as we get started on this journey together:

True transformation with lasting change requires rewiring. It requires you to consider different ideas and ways of thinking, to challenge existing beliefs, and to take action in different ways. Novelist Rita Mae Brown once wrote, "Insanity is doing the same thing over and over and expecting different results."[1] The same holds true here. You cannot change something in your life if you aren't willing to show up differently and try new things.

Transformation takes time. It's a never-ending process in a lot of ways—especially when you have a growth mindset and are open to new ideas and experiences. It can have points of rapid growth followed by times that feel like you're stuck (or vice versa). The journey is not linear. There are ups and downs, along with moving forward or backward. I encourage you to fall in love with the process. Give yourself grace when you're not feeling movement. Celebrate when you hit milestones or have breakthroughs. Welcome it all because, at the end of the day, that's what this life is for. It's for living, experiencing, and taking things moment by moment.

Personally, it took me years to shift from planning for the future to living more in the moment. It's not that I don't plan anything now, but I stop myself from looking steps ahead as much as I can. There is magic in being in the moment. It allows for less heartache when things don't happen as you may have wanted them to. It also allows you to see the beauty in unexpected opportunities by following high vibrational energy and listening to your body.

There are a few perspectives that have served me well in the transformation process. I'd like to share them with you up front with the hope that it makes it easier to take in the information and wisdom shared in this book.

In order to get the most out of this book, I invite you to:

Come with an open heart and an open mind. Be curious and open to different perspectives. You don't have to change what you believe (unless you want to, of course), but I invite you to explore new ways of thinking and being. That is truly where the magic happens. It may feel uncomfortable or scary to try new things and that's ok. Small steps can be just as impactful as big ones, if not more so. Maybe you'll read this book, but it will take you time to wrap your arms around it. That's ok too. You can come back anytime and allow it to support you on your journey.

Put yourself first in this process. When it comes to your own personal transformation and creating a life that you really want, you are in charge. Typically, people will try to take what they can from you / your relationship so it can best serve them. This doesn't have to be malicious or with ill intention, although it can be, of course. The point is, most people are looking out for themselves. This means you'll need to put yourself first in this process. That can look like carving out time to read this book, setting aside time to do the exercises mentioned, and making time for yourself every day. No one else is going to do this work for you, so you need to make sure you are showing up for yourself in any way that's possible for you to do so.

Ditch the worry about what others will think. Society tries to get us to conform to certain standards. It's more comfortable when we want the same things and to behave the same ways. We're conditioned by the world around us from childhood. If you're anything like me, you've worried a time or two (or 1,000) about what other people will think. The truth is, this life is your life. The things you want may not be what other people want. That is ok. It's part of what makes you unique on this planet. This journey is yours and yours alone. Block out the noise from others and do your thing.

Keep a journal. This book includes many prompts, reflection questions, and activities to support your personal transformation. Documenting your thoughts and feelings will allow you to process differently than keeping it all in your head. It can also serve as a nice memento of your process that you can look back on to see your growth and evolution. I also recommend keeping a notebook next to your bed for any early morning or late night reflections. You'll be surprised at what comes up in these pockets of time.

Anything you want is available to you if you choose it.

Are you ready to begin?

Part 1: Understanding the Mind-Body Connection

Introduction

The Mind-Body Connection is something that has fascinated me for years. Most of us walk around this planet with our heads down, focused on going through the motions. We go to work, think about what's for dinner, go home to cook, help kids with homework, watch TV, and go to bed. Then, we wake up the next day and do it all over again. It's a repetitive cycle we might not even realize we're in. It's time for us to wake up, connect within, and live our lives to the fullest.

The Mind-Body Connection is about how we bring awareness to both our mind and our body and allow them to work in harmony. Most of us are used to operating solely from the mind. We think, overanalyze, and allow our mind to direct us, dictating our thoughts and controlling our emotions. However, we are not our thoughts. We don't want the mind in the driver's seat of our life. When we connect more to our body and from there, our soul, we can operate from a very different perspective. We can see life with more love and acceptance. We can quiet the noise, comparison, and inadequacy our mind wants us to believe and feel more peace, ease, and joy. And we'll be able to fully embody our authentic selves.

You don't have to wait until you have a major life crisis or a health scare to start living your life more fully. (If you have already had one and that's why you picked up this book, that's ok too!)

Part 1 explores the Mind-Body Connection as a basis for true transformation and lasting change in your life. Using both lenses of science and spirituality, you'll learn there is always more to what's going on than what you may think.

The Science Of The
Mind-Body Connection

The Mind-Body Connection and Its Impact on Physical Health

Your mind and body work together to create what is happening in your life. Most people are reactive with their health. Meaning, when something appears as an ailment (i.e. a rash, sickness, broken bone, etc.), most people go to a doctor and get treatment. Once it's healed, they move on with their life and don't necessarily explore what may have caused the ailment to begin with. What many people don't realize is your thoughts and emotions have a physical manifestation in your body. When you are proactive with your health and manage your well-being, you have the potential to reduce the physical ailments that show up in your life.

Several studies have shown that the mind-body connection has the ability to impact physical health. This type of research is shedding a light on the fact that our minds are more powerful than we realize. I'm not saying that if we connect more deeply within, then all our problems and challenges will go away. However, we do get stronger and become more self aware. When that happens, we shift our perspective and move through the world differently. This may mean certain things are easier for you to navigate than they were in the past, or perhaps situations don't spiral out of control because you are more aware and able to manage expectations differently.

The following examples from Integris Health[1] highlight some of the research being done to recognize the correlation between the mind and body in medical patients and their healing.

- A researcher at the University of California at San Francisco found that breast cancer patients who participated in weekly group therapy sessions survived nearly twice as long as patients who did not participate.

- Researchers at Ohio State University have found that breast cancer patients with the greatest anxiety about their medical condition had the lowest levels of white blood cells that normally attack cancer and combat infection. In blood of women with high degrees of stress, there were 20 to 30 percent fewer natural killer cells that play key roles in the body's defenses. The study is the first part in a long-term project to test whether controlling stress can play a role in fighting cancer.

- At Harvard, studies have shown that meditation can help lower high blood pressure, decrease the level of chronic pain, and diminish nausea that accompanies chemotherapy.

- Researchers at the Mid America Heart Institute at St. Luke's Hospital in Kansas City found that heart patients who had someone praying for them -- without their knowledge -- suffered 10 percent fewer complications. Researchers came to the conclusion after studying 990 patients admitted during a year to the institute's coronary care unit. Half the patients were prayed for daily by community volunteers; the other patients did not have anyone assigned to pray for them. Patients, families and caregivers were not aware of the study. After four weeks, prayed-for patients had about 10 percent fewer complications such as chest pain and cardiac arrest, researchers reported in "Archives of Internal Medicine."

It's time for us to start paying attention and understand that our thoughts matter. We can change our own narratives. Once we understand that, we will reduce stress and anger. This will allow our bodies to meet us in a healthier place.

The Impact of Stress on the Body

According to the World Health Organization, "Stress can be defined as a state of worry or mental tension caused by a difficult situation. Stress is a natural human response that prompts us to address challenges and threats in our lives. Everyone experiences stress to some degree. The way we respond to stress, however, makes a big difference to our overall well-being."[2]

Stress is a feeling from the mind. It is not something tangible you can feel and touch. It is the compilation of thoughts and feelings overloading your system (mind and body). When that stress becomes too great without an outlet for release, it starts to manifest and show signs in the body.

This can show up in many ways including insomnia, headaches, teeth grinding, hypertension, fatigue, weight gain, digestive issues, etc. Ailments are how our bodies try to communicate with us that something is not right. A sign we are out of alignment with something in our lives. There are also emotional responses that affect physical well-being. This can include anxiety, depression, anger, fear, grief, and sadness. As well as chronic guilt, shame, resentment, or bitterness.

Oftentimes, people dismiss what's happening in their body as a random happenstance. As a society, we do not have a mentality that our bodies are incredibly powerful and a crucial part of our lives. Yes, they give us breath and it's how we are here on this planet, but it's also more than that. Our bodies are masterful systems that allow our soul to experience many things —walking, eating, talking, running, creating, etc. Without our bodies, what would we be?

This is an opportunity and an invitation to see your body in a different way. To appreciate it for its power and the wonder it brings to your life. Improving your mind-body connection does not have to be a hard, long, and complex process. There are many simple ways you can improve this connection and that's what you will learn about in this book.

How Feelings Show Up in the Body

Our emotions can take a toll on our bodies. We can usually recognize emotions showing up in our bodies. For example, when we're embarrassed, our cheeks get flushed, and when we're nervous, our palms get sweaty.

A Finnish study from 2013 mapped body reactions from about 700 people. They were able to see patterns of how feeling showed up in the body. "Emotions associated with fear, anger and anxiety showed increased sensations in the chest, face and upper body. These emotions were also found to get the body ready for quick action by increasing heart rate and tightening muscles."[3]

When you constantly feel certain emotions, you may have consistent feelings in the body around those emotions. For example, if you always feel stressed and it shows up as a tightening of your muscles, over time your muscles will get tighter and tighter. While having contracted muscles may not seem like a big deal, if you hold on to this tension instead of clearing it from your body, it can then start to show up in other parts of your body. You may get tension headaches or sore muscles and bones that make it painful to move in certain ways. Emotions can really find their way into your body and stay there, causing havoc on your nervous system.

For 20 years, I had a swelling in my left leg that would come and go. Sometimes it would stay for a long time (i.e. all 9 months of each of my pregnancies) and other times it would come and go within days. I went to many doctors and had multiple scans of my leg, yet nothing showed up as an issue.

That was until last year when I went to a new osteopath. An osteopath is a medical practitioner who "is trained to treat injuries to bones and muscles using pressure and movement."[4] Osteopaths are very popular in France, where I live, and people generally visit an osteopath 1 or 2 times a year.

The woman I went to see works with many modalities including osteopathy, acupuncture, kinesiology (working with body muscles), and more. Her intake process included questions about my overall health and habits, along with my emotions and well-being. As she started to look at my body, she noticed it was blocked in many places. As she unblocked these areas using a variety of techniques, she also asked me about my emotional health and my relationship with change. She asked about my childhood and different stories related to the big changes I went through in my life. I shared a few situations as well as my earliest memories of my leg being swollen 20 years prior.

All parts of the body have a connection to the mind and spiritual worlds. The left leg represents our relationship with the feminine aspect of self. In my case, she shared that I may be holding on to leftover resentment or an imbalance of some sort with the feminine side of myself. She encouraged me to keep track of any time I felt the swelling in my leg along with any emotions or events that were happening around this time.

After some internal work and further reflection, I identified a belief that I had been holding on to for most of my life. The belief that *change is hard*. And while, yes, change can be hard, it can also be easy. We are all continuously going through change and when we embrace it, we can arrive at new amazing places we never imagined.

As I explored this belief and questioned it further, I realized it was no longer serving me. I arrived at a place where I recognized the beauty of change, the possibilities it includes, and that while it can be hard, I will find a way through. I didn't have to hold on to that old belief anymore.

I decided to build a new relationship with this energy and with my left leg, and as the doctor requested, kept track of how the swelling associated with my emotions. I typically go for daily walks in nature. It's rare I miss a day because I enjoy it so much and it really connects me to my higher self. On my walk, I decided to talk to my leg. To explain to my leg that while it has kept me safe by storing my feelings of worry and stress over the years, it doesn't need to do that anymore. I have other tools I can use (including therapy, somatic exercises, and more) so the emotion does not need to be stored within me. I can allow it to move through me instead. I repeated that we are safe, that we have another way forward, and that the stored emotions can leave my body now. I shared what I've learned over the years and how I am showing up in a new way for myself and others.

A mantra that came to me on my walk was:

I am in perfect harmony with the divine feminine
and the divine masculine.

I repeated it out loud the rest of my way home. I knew in that moment my body was releasing old emotions and integrating a new form of being.

The swelling didn't leave my leg at that exact moment. However, over the next few days, it went down quite a bit. Now, anytime I feel stress and it tries to hold in my left leg, I do body exercises and speak to my leg and remind it that it doesn't need to store that feeling. We are safe and we are loved as we are.

Since the days after my walk and prayer, I haven't written any other entries.

There is a power in speaking to your body in a loving way. It listens to how you treat it, take care of it, and love it. This was a powerful lesson I will remember for the rest of my life and I'm so grateful to have had the experience.

I recognize it may sound crazy and that not everyone will believe this story. That's ok. I am sharing it as a way to open people to the possibility of deeper mind-body connections. Should you want to explore this deeper, you're invited to take a look at any chronic illnesses or pain that you have and explore your emotions that may be tied to it. Everything may not be fixed quickly and yet, what have you got to lose by trying?

How the Mind Tricks the Body: The Placebo Effect

A great example of the power of our minds is something called the "Placebo Effect". A placebo is "a substance that has no therapeutic effect."[5] In clinical trials while testing new medicines, the patients are divided into two groups. One group gets the actual drug intended for use. The other group gets a placebo, which does not include the medication. The patients do not know if they are receiving the active drug or the placebo. All of the patients are then followed and studied to monitor their symptoms and any improvement from the medication.

According to Harvard Medical School, "Measurable physiological changes can be observed in those taking a placebo, similar to those observed among people taking effective medications. In particular, blood pressure, heart rate, and various blood test results have been shown to change among subsets of research subjects who responded to a placebo."[6]

An article from Harvard Medical School explains that the

placebo effect is "about creating a stronger connection between the brain and body and how they work together."

"Even if they know it's not medicine, the action itself can stimulate the brain into thinking the body is being healed."[7] As these studies continue to evolve, scientists are able to show more correlations between the mind and body, how they work together, and how they impact each other.

Reflection 1.1

What is your relationship with your
mind-body connection at this time?

_____

_____

_____

_____

_____

_____

_____

_____

_____

_____

_____

_____

_____

_____

_____

_____

_____

_____

_____

_____

_____

_____

_____

_____

Healing Modalities

Holistic Healing Approaches

Throughout time, civilizations have shown us that there are many ways to heal using holistic medicine. While technology and science have evolved to provide us with more options to combat disease and illness, people are becoming more interested in holistic healing methods again.

Holistic healing looks at the whole human—mind, body, spirit, and emotions—in order to treat the whole person for optimal well-being. With this approach, it is considered that everything is deeply connected and intertwined. When one part of the person is out of balance, it can create an imbalance in other areas of the mind or body.

When you take a holistic approach to your health and well-being, you will start to notice the connections and cause and effect that live within you. Food is an easy example most people can see rather quickly. If you eat a certain food that doesn't agree with your system, you will see the negative impact on your digestive system.

When we pay attention to not only our mind, but our body, spirit, and emotions, it allows us to connect to our true nature. Bringing us more peace, joy, and fulfillment as we navigate the world around us.

Holistic healing takes into account the natural and integrative healing methods along with traditional Western medicine.

Throughout this book, you'll learn about various tools and approaches that integrate both Western and Eastern philosophies. You can look at it as taking the best of both worlds for a well-rounded approach to your overall well-being.

Over the years, the Western world has moved to a more medically focused approach to life. We react to our ailments by taking medication and numbing our pain. As someone that spent over a decade of her career in the pharmaceutical industry, I'm a firm believer that there is a time and place for medicine. Each of us can decide for ourselves what is in our best interest. At the same time, the Western healthcare system is not always focusing on the root cause and treating the whole human. With a medically focused direction, many natural remedies have been dismissed as invaluable or not beneficial. We've headed down a path that has lost its connection to mother nature and the notion that we are all connected as one.

I am not saying that only natural remedies are the way to go. Modern medicine has made many great advancements in our time, and yet there are powerful resources within the Eastern approach to health and well-being that would benefit us if we re-incorporate them into our lives.

In a world that wants everyone to live in extremes, I invite you to get curious. This book will continue to show you that life is what you make it. It is up to YOU to decide how you want to live. I'm merely shedding a light on how you can wake yourself up to your own internal mind-body connection and change the course of your existence to align with who you really are.

The Power of Cognitive Behavioral Therapy

Cognitive Behavioral Therapy (CBT) is a modality that explores your mind and thought patterns. It includes a process for identifying and observing your negative thought patterns and behaviors in order to replace them with something more supportive to you. CBT mainly focuses on what is happening in the present so you can see how it is impacting your daily life and make changes to support the life you want to live.

According to the American Psychological Association, CBT "has been demonstrated to be effective for a range of problems including depression, anxiety disorders, alcohol and drug use problems, marital problems, eating disorders, and severe mental illness." [1]

For those of us that are really caught up in the mind and like to overanalyze, Cognitive Behavioral Therapy can be a great place to start exploring your thoughts.

The fundamental concepts of CBT include:

- identifying and changing negative thought patterns,
- developing problem-solving skills, and
- engaging in behavioral experiments to test the validity of automatic thoughts. [2]

For a long time, I thought only people with very deep-rooted issues would see a therapist. I couldn't tell you what those deep-rooted issues were, but in my mind, therapy was for people that needed 'help' and I didn't need help.

That all changed when my family moved to France for my husband's job. I realized I would need someone to process all of my feelings with, and that person couldn't be one of my closest loved ones or friends. Loved ones and friends can be great support systems, and yet I didn't want or expect my family or friends to consistently support me in that way. I wanted to speak with a professional that would show up and hold space to support me in what I was navigating while giving me tools to continue to work through things on my own.

I came to realize that a therapist is an ally. They can teach you how to reframe your thoughts and help you spot patterns to choose a different path forward. Having a therapist was instrumental for me to make it through our international move with more ease and grace for myself while also being able to support my daughters with the transition. As parents and caregivers, we tend to hold a lot of our family's dynamics in our hearts. It's important that if you play that role in your family, you also have an outlet to get your own support. None of us can do all of this alone. We're not meant to. Finding the right support for yourself is a critical step.

If you've never explored therapy before and are curious about it, the first step is finding the right therapist. There are many out there, but not all of them will feel like a fit for you. Depending on where you live and your access to insurance, you can call your insurance provider to get a list of approved therapists. From there, I recommend meeting with at least 2-3 therapists to see which one feels like the best fit for you. Don't be afraid to recognize if someone isn't a fit. You don't need a specific reason. If you don't feel like you're connecting, it's better to try meeting with someone else.

Therapy tends to be a taboo topic, especially in older generations. I'm happy to see that in recent years, more and more people are speaking out about mental health and the benefits of therapy. Olympic Gold Medal Gymnast Simone Biles, Tennis Pro Naomi Osaka, and Basketball Legend Lebron James have all spoken out about the importance of taking care of your mental health.[3] We still have a long way to go, but the more we allow and encourage open conversations around therapy and its benefits, the more healing can occur throughout the world.

Note: We have a long way to go in having equitable healthcare for all and I recognize therapy is not accessible or affordable to everyone. I hope you are able to find the support you need, whether that is from your medical insurance or from networks and organizations that provide counseling services to those in need.

The Holistic Nature of Somatic Therapy

Somatic Therapy is a therapeutic approach that focuses on the mind-body connection. The aim is to heal from emotional, mental, and physical trauma through awareness of the body. In Somatic Therapy, it is believed that unresolved emotions, stress, and trauma get stored in the body and create symptoms that are manifested via the body.

Movement is a way to process and release the energy of stored emotions instead of holding on to it. Children embrace a natural tendency to move around and be active. This is their body's way of managing and releasing the energy that moves through them. As we get older, we tend to have more sedentary lifestyles. Technology finds most of us sitting and using a computer for most of the workday, with little time spent outdoors or moving around.

If we aren't moving around, where does our energy go? Without properly processing our emotions and our energy, we end up storing our emotions in our bodies. Somatic Therapy is a way to incorporate movement and body awareness into your life as a way to release those emotions.

My Experience With The Mind-Body Connection

A few years ago, I started body tapping as a way to release stored emotions in my body. Simple daily exercises slowly released stored stressors—past emotions and feelings I unknowingly held on to—from my body. I even managed to stop grinding my teeth at night (a stress induced habit) by doing daily toe tapping exercises before bed. I'll speak more about my experiences with tapping and stored emotions in Part 4: The Body, however, it's worth noting here. The possibilities for healing are endless.

The areas in your body that bring pain or discomfort are all areas for potential healing. From there, you can find ways to release the stored emotions clogging up your system. Releasing the stored emotions will allow you to open up and go more deeply within your soul—to access the higher parts of yourself.

Personally, I've found a combination of Cognitive Behavioral Therapy and Somatic Therapy to be the most transformative. These two approaches incorporate rewiring negative thought patterns while also releasing stored emotions. When you get out of your head and into your body, you start to tune into what your body is trying to tell you.

Part 1: Key Takeaways

Understanding The Mind-Body Connection

- A holistic healing approach considers the whole of who you are—not only one part of you.

- Eastern and Western medicinal practices both offer wisdom we can learn and benefit from.

- Cognitive Behavioral Therapy is one approach you can use to identify and rewire negative thought patterns.

- Somatic Therapy is one approach you can use to release stored emotions and trauma from your body.

- Expanding your awareness to include both medical and natural healing modalities can bring more balance into your life.

Reminder:

Stay open and curious on your journey.

Part 2:
The Whole Self

My Story

In early 2018, I woke up one morning with a feeling that all of my teeth were falling out. I ran to the mirror to see if everything looked in order. Were my teeth still there? Yes, thankfully! But I couldn't see anything that would explain why I had so much pain in my mouth. I called my dentist and made an emergency dental appointment—a first for me. When I went in for an evaluation, he noticed signs of grinding. It turned out, I was grinding my teeth at night and the pain from grinding had now showed up in my waking life. The typical reason for grinding teeth at night is stress related, I was told.

During that time, I was under enormous stress and pressure. I was navigating a corporate job that required a lot of travel. Being away from home roughly 3 out of every 4 weeks during the first quarter of that year. I had two children under the age of 5. I was also building my product business at night and on the weekends, hoping it would grow into something bigger. It was a lot. Added to that, I had a newer boss that wanted the team to be on the road as much as possible instead of only when it was necessary.

Needless to say, it was a less than ideal situation and it finally caught up with me. This was the first time I truly understood that my body was showing me what was going on in my mind. Unfortunately, I became painfully aware of the mind-body connection with this experience. I was not in alignment.

I was carrying too much on my shoulders, and it was not sustainable. I had been unhappy with my job for a while and was considering if or when I could leave to build my product business full time. That time had come. Over the previous year, my husband and I had many conversations, and we made a plan for my exit from Corporate America. In April 2018, I became a full-time entrepreneur.

Becoming an entrepreneur invites you into a deep discovery to learn more about yourself—more so than a corporate job does. When you're responsible for your salary, if you feel motivated or not, how you want to work, etcetera; it changes the game. You need to look internally to really see how you tick and how to get through your blocks. If you don't get through the blocks, your next level of growth won't come. Whereas, with a corporate job, you can generally show up and collect a paycheck. It doesn't require as much of an internal look at yourself (although it can). Having a new found awareness for the mind-body connection along with being a business owner set me on a path of deep self-discovery.

I've spent my whole life studying people and systems along with a 20+ year career centered around change—whether it was helping departments create better systems or working with individuals to learn more about themselves. I've served companies as both a senior level leader and as an external consultant to bring different perspectives and new ways of doing things. I've run my own product business as well as a community for mom business owners supporting their growth and connections.

My life experiences have intertwined in some pretty incredible ways. From a love of math and science that got me an engineering degree, to seeing my grandfather's ghost at 16. You could say I've always felt I straddled two worlds—the incredibly practical earth our feet stand on, along with the air of the spiritual world that is always guiding us with signs and signals. I truly believe the universe is always conspiring for our highest good—whether that is with an incredible opportunity or a hard lesson to learn.

I grew up listening to stories of synchronicities from my dad. This is not something most people can say. For example, he had a bad feeling about getting into his friend's car, so he didn't go with him. His friend's car ended up crashing and a telephone pole landed on the seat where my dad would have been sitting. When my dad was older, he had premonitions about planes crashing that actually came true, and he even had a vision of one of my siblings breaking their arm. That vision also came true. Living at a time when spiritual or paranormal type of happenings were not talked about, my dad had some pretty lonely experiences and wasn't able to process them until later in life. I'm proud to say I grew up with these stories weaving into my reality. Perhaps this is part of why I am so open to possibilities and spirituality. When I went to our car one night to get something and saw my grandfather's ghost, I was scared, but I had my dad to run to and talk through it with. Looking back, I can see so clearly how these experiences shaped me and how they had a role in writing this book.

It took me a long time to understand and accept that this is the way I am. I am of both the Earth and the Sky. I embody the masculine and the feminine. I am a bridge that connects the mind and body in a way that accesses spirit. This is a gift to the world and when I embrace it, magic happens.

I did not reach this realization out of the blue. I came to this understanding over time and with a lot of experimentation. I've researched and experimented with many healing modalities—Cognitive Behavioral Therapy, energy and bodywork, and new experiences. These experiences included swimming across a freezing lake and saying a prayer under a waterfall, traveling to

Egypt and feeling the energy of the pyramids, seeing spirits called into a village in Zimbabwe, and so much more. I've done body tapping to release stored emotions and taken walks in nature almost every single day for almost two years. These experiences have shaped me in so many ways. They've allowed me to open and see more of myself. In turn, it has showed me the many ways that each and every one of us can access our own mind-body connection.

There are many ways to arrive at your highest alignment. It requires you to show up and find what works for you. Life is not one size fits all (as much as people like to tell you that). You have to create what you want. You have to find what works for you and your life. Walks in nature and being among the trees are one of my favorite things to do, but maybe yours is to paint, dance, or sit in a quiet room and meditate. We can all access more of our own alignment by feeling into what we love to do and following that feeling of love. When you get grounded and quiet your mind to connect with your body, you'll be able to tap into your true essence—your soul.

My hope is that this book supports you in seeing your gifts. That it allows you to open yourself up to new possibilities. That you may feel more at ease and grounded by implementing simple tools into your day-to-day life.

Understanding
The Whole Self

The first step on this journey is evaluating where you are now. Measuring where you are currently will help you see your growth and transformation more clearly. Through conditioning, old family patterns, and your own life experiences, you may not have ever really celebrated your true self. Or given yourself credit for how far you've come and where you are today. Let's start with the you that you may not have been able to acknowledge.

What are 1–3 things you are proud of?

_____

_____

_____

_____

What are you celebrating from your life so far?

_____

_____

_____

_____

_____

What are 3–5 of your strengths?

_____

_____

_____

_____

_____

What is your superpower? It may be something that comes so naturally to you that you don't think twice about it.

_____

_____

_____

_____

I encourage you to journal or meditate around the answers to these questions. Take time to discover more about who you are in this moment. You can also revisit these prompts throughout your journey to tweak and update them. As you move through this book, there will be more activities and tools to support you in deepening your practices. You are ever changing, so the answers to some of these questions may change as you work toward becoming more of who you truly are.

The first two questions that are asked in the Kaballah are: *Who are you?* and *What do you want?* For a long time, I struggled to answer these questions. I was listening so much to the world around me that I struggled to hear the answers that were deep inside me. It's difficult to break old habits or break free from the thoughts of others to really stand in your power. I encourage you to sit with these questions as part of your self-discovery process.

It's time to realize your personal power and to believe in yourself. All the answers to your desires are already in you. There is no need to look outside. A combination of support to help you reflect (i.e. this book) along with listening to your inner knowing, is how you will reach the answers to these questions faster.

Embracing
Self-Responsibility

S elf-responsibility is the act of taking responsibility for your own actions. It's about admitting the role you play in your life. If you've played the victim or have had a tendency to blame others for your struggles in the past, it's time to claim ownership. It's time to recognize you have agency over your life. You are the one that can heal and free yourself from limiting beliefs to achieve your greatest expansion. No one else can do this for you.

In relational dynamics with family and friends, people may fall into a pattern known as the Karpman Drama Triangle. Developed by psychiatrist Stephen B. Karpman in 1968, the Drama Triangle has three roles that are used fluidly and switched between the actors taking on these roles—the victim, the rescuer, and the persecutor. The victim represents someone that is acting like a victim in a given scenario. The rescuer takes on the role of 'saving the day' and feels guilty if they do not help the victim. The persecutor (a.k.a. the villain) insists that it's all the fault of the other person.[1]

In this Drama Triangle, we may take on different roles and play them out in different ways, depending on the situation. The invitation and the reason I am sharing the Drama Triangle with you now is for you to reflect on any ways you may have taken on any of these roles in your relationships.

Self-responsibility requires us to be honest about the roles we are playing, how it contributes to where we are now, and how it may block us from getting to where we want to be. Through your self-awareness and realizations, you will see a different path forward for your self. A way to take control of your life and create what you really want.

The key to making any type of transformation or change is to first understand where you are in this moment. A healthy dose of self-awareness is critical for this step in the process. It's a time to be honest with yourself: Are you a victim, rescuer, or persecutor?

What in your life is working right now?

_____

_____

_____

_____

_____

_____

What in your life is NOT working right now? Why?

_____

_____

_____

_____

_____

_____

How have you contributed to where you are?

_____

_____

_____

_____

_____

_____

How are you getting in the way of where you want to be?

_____

_____

_____

_____

_____

_____

_____

This work requires you to get vulnerable and meet yourself where you are. There is no more hiding. It's time to heal. It's time to expand. It's time to change your life.

As you take this journey, you will raise your energy to higher vibrations and pull yourself out of the low expressions that may keep you down today. As the shift from low to high expression develops and strengthens, you will begin to see a completely different way of operating in your life.

Note: This information is not meant to be taken lightly. Family dynamics can create deep cycles within these patterns and it is best to consult a healthcare professional if you need to go deeper into this methodology as part of your healing.

There may be circumstances in your life that are/were extremely hard or challenging to navigate, and I recognize you may have situations that are beyond your control. The type of responsibility I'm speaking about here is where you've had agency over your life and an ability to make your own decisions.

Reflection 2.1

Self-Awareness

Self-reflection is an effective way to start practicing self-awareness, and awareness is the first step in making bigger changes in
your life. To get started, reflect on and answer these questions
every evening before going to sleep.

Observe your answers to these prompts and see how they shift
for you over time. In time, you'll be able to look back through
your reflections to see how you've grown, changed, and evolved.

You're invited to consider the following questions on a daily basis:

What is at least 1 thing you are celebrating today?

_____

_____

_____

_____

_____

_____

Where did you show up for yourself today?

_____

_____

_____

_____

_____

_____

Did you have any challenges today? If so, how
did you handle them?

_____

_____

_____

_____

_____

Is there something you wish you would have
done differently today?

_____

_____

_____

_____

_____

_____

Taking Care Of
Your Whole Self

Practicing Self-Love

Do you love yourself? I don't mean tolerate or even like yourself. I mean, *love* yourself deeply in your bones. Do you recognize and appreciate what a unique individual you are?

Do you love yourself more than anyone or anything else in the world? Do you take care of yourself the same way you'd take care of others—whether it's your children, best friend, or partner?

I teach my daughters to love themselves first. Why? Because no one will love you as much as you love yourself, or at least not in the same way. It's important to love yourself deeply, more than anyone else in your life.

I know it's not easy. The way society is running at the moment, it's probably easier to *not* love yourself than to actually love yourself. It can feel easy to put ourselves down or focus on how we wish we were different. Along with that, our brains are programmed to have negativity bias (more on this in Part 3: The Mind).

You are miraculous. Your body and your mind and soul are gifts to this world.

Practicing Self-Care

Oftentimes, we skip out on taking care of ourselves because there are so many people around us that need us. It's easier to say we'll do something for ourselves later. We're too busy. There's too much going on. The reality is, we need to put ourselves first. There's a saying that you can't pour from an empty cup. This serves as a good reminder that you need to take care of yourself in order to take care of others.

I know self-care is seen as a buzzword these days. It's usually meant for massages, lattes, or other things to treat yourself. That's great because it's important to have rituals that support you. The self-care I'm talking about, though, isn't related to the material aspect of self-care. It's how you show up when you have to make a decision between yourself and someone else. It's how you make a decision that feels most correct to you without feeling guilty or wrong in your decision.

As a mom, I always felt it was easy to neglect myself because my kids always came first. It took me years to realize I'm a better parent if I put myself first. Now, I make it a priority to take solo walks and have time to myself daily. It really serves everyone in the house, not just me. It gives me more patience and under-standing, which allows me to show up as a healthier version of myself. When I take care of my well-being, it sends positive ripples out to the rest of my family.

It can be easy to list all the things we think are 'wrong' with us, but if I asked you, *What do you love about yourself?* Would you have an answer? Could you list more than one thing? All our experiences in relationships actually begin with how we feel about ourselves on the inside and how much we love ourselves.

You're invited to reflect on the following questions:

- Do you carve out time for yourself on a regular basis?
- How often do you say positive things to yourself?
- What are 10 things you love about yourself?

_____

_____

_____

_____

_____

_____

_____

_____

_____

_____

If you are someone that beats yourself up a lot for mistakes you make or blames yourself when things don't go the way you planned, can you reframe that negative self-talk? Can you rephrase it or bring another perspective to the situation? For example, instead of blaming yourself for a mistake, can you tell yourself, *I did the best I could in that situation with what I knew at the time?* Another option could be asking yourself, *What did I learn in this situation that I will take with me for next time?* As you practice this, you will begin to rewire your brain. It will have a ripple effect for you in your relationships—both your relationship with yourself and with others.

How you treat yourself on the inside matters deeply. You can do all the self-care activities—going for massages, meditation, etc., but if you aren't also working to reframe your thoughts, the change won't last in the same way.

I have a friend, Amy* (name changed), that struggles with self-care. She is always giving to everyone else, and she has a hard time putting her needs first. This had led her to burnout a few times already.

She knows I'm pretty diligent with my self-care routines, as it's a big part of my work. I move my body daily, generally eat in a balanced way, and I go to sleep on the early side. She has always admired this, but wasn't sure how to do it for herself. One day, she was really struggling and decided she was going to pretend to be me. She was about to start working again at 11 p.m. and she asked herself, *"What would Mary do in this instance?"* She reflected and said, *"Well, Mary would prioritize sleep and start work again tomorrow instead of trying to power through."* She ended up going to bed and getting a good night's sleep so she could face the next day with energy and focus. Now it's a joke for us, but in the moment, it really did help her.

I share this as an example for you to see that you can frame things however you want to shift your mindset. Do I think she should always use me as her benchmark? Absolutely not. It's best for her to do what works best for her. However, if this funny example gives her a jumpstart on her path and gets her used to thinking about herself differently, that's a great place to start. You can absolutely be creative with the ways you motivate yourself in order to take care of yourself first.

You're invited to reflect on the following questions:

- Do you love yourself?
- How much do you love yourself?
- How often do you remind yourself of this love?

_____

_____

_____

_____

_____

_____

_____

_____

_____

_____

When you are going through a tough time and need a reminder of your love, there is a simple exercise you can do. Cross your arms over your chest and hold on to your shoulders on either side so you're giving yourself a hug. Tell yourself, _I love myself,_ and give yourself a hug. Say _I love myself_ over and over and over, however many times you need to. I showed this to my daughters and then a few days later, one of them was going through something hard and she did this exercise. It was really beautiful to witness.

It's important to find ways you can remind yourself how to connect deeper down and navigate your life with more love for yourself. At the end of the day, the person you have throughout your whole life is you. Relationships come and go. Family members and friends all come and go, but you always have yourself. So, how are you loving yourself today?

How can it be part of your everyday thinking so it becomes a nonissue, a nonnegotiable? Yes, I love myself. I love myself to the max, and I treat myself with care. In order to strengthen this connection, we can look at some of the practical ways we show up daily.

5 Pillars Of Self-Care

Most people think they need to do something drastic in order to change their life. And while yes, that is possible, there are also simpler ways to change that can have a great impact (with less pain and heartache, I might add). Hustle culture may have us thinking we always need to push through to achieve our goals or live our dream life. The truth is, you can also achieve this through softening to the process and being open to making small changes that collectively have a big impact.

The habits I'm going to share here are simple; anyone can do them. However, they may not always feel easy to implement. They are all things I've found have worked wonders in strengthening the mind-body connection for myself as well as my clients.

Remember, in order to change your life, you have to be willing to do things differently. That may mean experimenting with some of these habits. You might already have a few of these in place, or maybe you don't have any in place. Wherever you are is ok. What's important is what you choose to do about it.

My recommendation is to start with one item on the list. See how you can incorporate more of it into your life regularly. As you get used to it and find a new routine, then add another habit into the mix. Life is ever evolving and taking care of yourself is a foundational step.

Pillar 1: Are you getting a good night of sleep?

Sleep is a critical part of our well-being and it is often overlooked or treated as an afterthought of taking care of yourself. We're often trained to push through, be more productive, and get as much done as we can. As a society, rest is not particularly honored or appreciated. Some of the many benefits of rest include: regulation of your mood, improvement of your immune system, regulation of your cortisol levels, stress relief, and improved mental function.[1] When you don't have enough sleep, you may feel extra irritable, tired, or crave sugary foods. Lack of sleep can also lead to chronic health complications, such as heart disease, kidney disease, high blood pressure, diabetes, and depression.[2]

Children aren't the only ones that need a full night of sleep. The average adult needs 7-9 hours of sleep per night.[3] Do you have a consistent sleep pattern? Do you know how many hours of sleep you need per night to feel rested? If you aren't sure, test out your sleep patterns over a period of time to see what works best for you. From there, you can decide what time to go to bed based on what time you need to wake up the next morning. Be sure to revisit your sleep schedule every so often. If you have young kids in the house, your sleep schedule may look very different versus when they are teenagers and getting themselves ready in the morning.

From a holistic and energetic perspective, I find sleep is a time that allows your body to heal and restore itself from the day. You dream space is a powerful time for your subconscious to work through issues from the day that may have been challenging. It can also be an opportunity for deep healing. I have had dreams that helped me heal my extreme fear of heights. I went from not being able to ride a ski lift or climb tall staircases to riding in a hot-air balloon over the Valley of the Kings and Queens in Luxor, Egypt (more on this in Part 3: The Mind).

Pillar 2: Are you keeping your body hydrated?

Our bodies are made up of up to 78% water.[4] This makes replenishing our bodies with water an important part of our daily habits. Water has the ability to hydrate our bodies while soda, alcohol, coffee, and other caffeinated beverages dehydrate us.

According to the Mayo Clinic, "Water is your body's principal chemical component and makes up about 50% to 70% of your body weight. Your body depends on water to survive."[5]

Generally, an adult female needs about 11.5 cups (2.7 liters) of water per day and an adult male needs about 15.5 cups (3.7 liters) per day. Not all of a person's water needs to come from drinking liquids, since some foods also contain water. "About 20% of daily fluid intake usually comes from food and the rest from drinks."[6]

Water serves as a essential part of our body's function. It's a vital nutrient to the life of every cell in our body, so it acts as a building material. Water also regulates our internal body temperature by sweating, acting as a shock absorber for the brain, spinal cord, and fetus. It forms saliva (which we need to eat), it lubricates joints, and it assists in flushing out waste through our system (mainly through urination).[7]

Keep in mind that alcohol and caffeinated drinks can take away from water's replenishing nature by dehydrating you. When you're thirsty, that is your body's way of telling you it needs more water. Drinking water regularly throughout the day is a great habit to keep, so even if you drink other liquids, you're still getting water into your body. Personally, before I drink a cup of tea in the morning, I drink a cup of water to make sure my body is still getting the nutrients it needs.

You can get creative about how you manage your water intake. There are water bottles you can purchase that measure out your needed water intake for the day. You can fill it once and focus on drinking that throughout the day. Find what works for you.

Pillar 3: Are you eating food that feels nourishing to you?

Along with water, food is a critical part of what keeps our bodies nourished and working properly. I recognize people have very strong beliefs around food and nutrition. Many also have emotions tied in as well. I like to keep things simple with food.

The way I approach food is to generally eat more whole foods (fruits and vegetables) and less processed foods (chips, cookies, ready-made meals, etc). This does not mean I don't eat these things—chocolate chip cookies are my favorite! However, I've found over the years that the healthier I eat, the clearer I feel in my mind and my body. There are chemicals and additives in processed food to make it last longer. When possible, I prefer to eat things that may not have as long of an expiration date, but that won't stay stuck in my body either. I still love sweets and dessert (including ice cream), but after paying more attention to my body and how it feels, I decided to cut down on my sugar intake to help my body avoid the sugar highs and lows.

Pillar 3 isn't meant to shame you for whatever you eat. What we eat and our relationship with food impacts our mind-body connection. When you pay attention to nutrition in this way, you'll feel lighter and more energized. You'll likely lessen or avoid gastrointestinal problems and sugar cravings as well.

I noticed a big difference in food culture and my relationship with food when my family moved from the United States to France. Local, fresh produce is prioritized in France. Every village has at least one farmers market per week. There are many initiatives across the country to eat locally and seasonally. The first couple of years living here, I found it hard to get used to the fact that the supermarket didn't have all of my favorite vegetables fully stocked year-round. Now that we've lived here a few years, I'm much more accustomed to the seasonal eating habits and I've found it to be better on my body.

As it turns out, eating seasonally is better for your body and for the environment. Eating local produce that is in season has the highest level of nutrients in the food. From a farming perspective, it is also better for the land, as it requires less energy to grow the crops and it creates sustainable eating patterns.[8]

Eat in ways that feel nourishing to you. Take into consideration how you feel both in your mind and body.

Note: Being able to eat seasonally depends on where you live and what is available. I also recognize this is a privilege to eat seasonally. As much as you can find choices for yourself, keep in mind that fruits and vegetables provide more nutrients that your body needs versus processed foods that contain a lot of salt and sugar. Make sure you are getting the nutrients you need and consult your healthcare professional if you have any doubts.

Pillar 4: Are you moving your body regularly?

Movement is critical to our health. When we move, our body produces endorphins, which play an important role in our bodies. When our body feels pain, our nerves send pain signals to our brain. This causes our brain to release endorphins that block the nerve cells that receive pain signals. Endorphins have an added benefit of improving our mood and reducing stress. If our bodies don't produce enough endorphins, it may lead to depression, anxiety, body aches, or even addiction.[9]

There are infinite ways to move your body. I'm of the mindset that it doesn't matter how you move your body as long as you move it. You can walk, stretch, play sports, practice yoga, dance, run, jump around, garden, hike—as long as it's getting you to move instead of sitting still, it counts. Moving your body stimulates your brain, reduces stress, replenishes your energy, lowers your risk of heart disease, and has many other benefits. With the increase of technology and remote work, it's easier than ever to be seated for most of the day. This makes it even more important to be aware of how much you move (or don't) and make an effort to increase your mobility.

It's recommended to walk at least 10,000 steps a day. A while back, I purchased a pedometer to track my steps for the day. Because I work from home, I wasn't sure how much I was actually moving on a given day. Having a pedometer allowed me to get an idea of my average daily steps (only about 5,000-6,000 steps). Then, I worked toward increasing my steps over time by getting outside, taking longer walks, sometimes walking faster to get more steps in within the same distance, or walking to pick up my kids from school instead of with the car.

Moving your body while spending time outside with trees, plants, flowers, and wildlife has the extra benefit of getting you grounded and connected with yourself. It is a great way to decompress and relax your nervous system. For me personally, when I go for walks in nature, I don't talk on my phone or listen to music. I take the time to pay attention to everything around me. It's amazing how nourishing plants and animals are when you take the time to be in the moment.[10]

Pillar 5: Are there unhealthy habits you'd like to eliminate in your life?

We all have our vices. Whether it's alcohol, nicotine, or doom scrolling (to name a few), there is always something around us that makes us feel good in the moment, but we know isn't healthy in the long run. These are all ways we may numb our pain. Let's be honest, doing the work to heal and grow can feel exhausting and sometimes even impossible. That's why a lot of people don't even try. However, you're reading this book, so that's not you. You know there is something else out there for you and you're willing to dig deeper.

Alcohol, nicotine, and screen time all have negative impacts on our health and well-being. Alcohol interferes with the brain's communication pathways, which can impact how the brain works. "Drinking alcohol is associated with risks of developing noncommunicable diseases such as liver diseases, heart diseases, and different types of cancers, as well as mental health and behavioural conditions such as depression, anxiety and alcohol use disorders."[11] As I get older, even one drink can impact my sleep and leave me feeling groggy the next day.

"Any use of nicotine can cause harmful effects on the body, including: high blood pressure, respiratory infections, gastroin-testinal problems, lung injury and exposure to metals and toxic solvents (through vaping)." Cigarette smoking is the leading cause of preventable disease. Some diseases that people suffer from related to nicotine products include: cancer, heart disease, stroke, diabetes, lung disease, and more.[12]

While I don't smoke and rarely drink, I am definitely guilty of doom scrolling and spending too much time on screens. It's something I'm consistently working at and some days I'm better at limiting my time than others.

Some things I like to do to limit screen time are:

- Setting a timer on my phone—especially for social media apps. You'd be surprised how quickly scrolling Instagram for 30 minutes can pass.

- Creating a bedtime routine that limits screen time before bed. For example, putting your phone in another room and reading a book before bed.

- Read, meditate, or tap before bed to prepare for a good night of sleep (More on meditation and tapping in Part 3: The Mind)

As an added tip, unfollow accounts that aren't supportive to your growth. What we consume online impacts our mental health. Be diligent and discerning about what you let into your world. While I don't think it's wise to be completely oblivious to the world around us, social media algorithms don't allow for us to consume content in a way that is healthy for us. They are designed to keep you on the platform longer and longer. Along with that, new tactics such as *rage bait*, where people purposely post controversial content to elicit reactions and make people angry (yes, really), are on the rise.

Regardless of what habits you may have (including ones not listed above), please know this isn't meant to shame you in any way. It's meant to highlight some areas we can almost always benefit from changing our relationship with over time.

Addressing Blocks To
Living As Your Whole Self

Identify Your Fears and Doubts

There are endless ways the mind can play tricks on us and make us believe we should be farther along or somewhere else completely. Our minds try to keep us stuck by allowing fears and doubts to take over. As a part of practicing self-love, it's important to highlight some of the ways you might be hurting yourself and preventing your growth and expansion in the process. The sooner you realize this is happening, the more you can reflect on it with self-awareness and compassion to begin the healing process.

Doubt and Overthinking

Doubt can cause you to worry about everything in a way that makes you fearful of taking your next step. Questioning if something is the right decision to make or overthinking every interaction can keep you stuck. This has shown up for me personally throughout the years, as well as for many of my clients.

Not Feeling Certain

Your mind may want you to have certainty and be 100% sure before taking action. It will want you to keep looking for more information before making a decision, which inevitably leads you to not deciding or taking action.

Hiding Your Voice

You may not feel comfortable or safe to speak up because you don't want to make waves. You may feel scared to voice your opinions or upset others. It may be more comfortable to hide in the shadows. This then prevents you from sharing your thoughts, opinions, and wisdom, all of which are gifts to the world.

Feeling Like You Don't Have a Purpose

You may feel lost. Maybe you're looking for a purpose and you're not sure who you are, who you're meant to be, or where you're going. Constantly telling yourself that you don't have a direction won't help you find your direction.

Pushing to Keep Up with Others

You may be pushing and trying to keep up with others, even when you're tired. The fear of missing out (FOMO) is real, but it only keeps you in low expressions of lack and insecurity. Go at your own rhythm and you'll accomplish so much more.

Needing to Prove Yourself

You may feel that you can't slow down because you need to prove yourself and what you're capable of. This simply isn't true. Honor yourself and who you are.

Holding onto Your Fears

You may be clinging to your fears as a way to stop yourself from moving forward. Change can be scary, especially when facing the unknown. When you hold on to those fears too tightly, they prevent you from taking even one step.

Worrying About What Other People Think

Fear of judgment from others is a very real fear. You could be worried about upsetting other people or worrying about what other people will think and allowing that to make you pause. We worry about what others will say or think about us. In the end, everyone has their own opinion—the only one that matters for you is your own.

Feeling Like You're Not Where You Should Be

You could feel like you're behind and you'll never really catch up. This could be that you're telling yourself you should have already been somewhere and you're not there yet.

These thoughts are meant to make you feel stuck and stay stuck. Finding yourself, finding your direction, and deciding your next move (for whatever situation you're in) is dependent upon how you navigate these types of scenarios. I invite you to consider the following:

- Do you often worry and overthink?

- Are you constantly seeking more information to be more certain?

- Are you hiding your voice and not speaking up?

- Do you feel like you don't have a direction in life and don't know what to do next?

- Do you keep pushing yourself too far and overdoing it?

- Are you trying to prove yourself in some way because you feel you're not good enough?

- Are you letting your fears stop you from trying new things?

- Are you worrying too much about what other people think?

- Do you feel pressure that you aren't where you're supposed to be?

These thoughts and feelings exist on a spectrum. Some may resonate more than others. It's important to identify where you get stuck. The way to identify where you get stuck is to dig deeper into what keeps you stuck and release yourself from it.

Reflection 2.2

What are the fears you hold on to the
most? How do they impact you?

_____

_____

_____

_____

_____

_____

_____

_____

_____

Overcoming Your Fears and Doubts

Becoming aware of your fears and doubts will put you on a path toward healing them. The healing journey becomes easier to move through when you have compassion for yourself. When you look at things that haven't worked out the way you wanted them to, do you see them as a failure or do you have compassion for yourself?

When things don't go as planned, I like to look at those experiences as lessons and redirections instead of failures or mistakes. It's easy to beat ourselves up and get frustrated when things don't work out, but that's what we're here on Earth to do. To test things out, explore, wonder, experiment, try new things, mess up, and pick ourselves up and try again. It's called the Game of Life for a reason.

The next time you find yourself steeped in negative self-talk, practice self-compassion and rephrase the negative self-talk to affirmations instead. Some go to's I like to use are:

- I am learning.

- This is part of the process.

- I learned that I like ____.

- I learned that I don't like ____.

- I have control over my thoughts and feelings.

- I am smart, and I am figuring things out.

Life is a marathon, not a sprint. Even though hustle culture will tell you otherwise, you do not need to have it all figured out by a certain age or on a certain timeline. You are exactly where you need to be in this moment. Along with self-compassion, remember to give yourself grace in this process. It takes time and practice to rewire and reframe your mindset. There will be days when you feel on top of the world and that you did an amazing job showing up for yourself. There will be other days when you feel you're right back where you started or moving backward in some way. I find that hormones, seasons, and many other factors can contribute to how we feel with our progress from one day to the next. It's important to remember to keep going, to trust in yourself, and to trust the direction you're moving in. Whether you can see ten steps ahead of you or only the step you're on, it doesn't matter as long as you're tuned into and connected with yourself.

Coming Back To Your Whole Self When You Feel Lost

When you feel lost, off track, or overwhelmed, it is time to look inward and reflect. If spending time on your own makes you restless—lean into that feeling. Allow yourself to get uncomfortable. To explore and get to know yourself. Embrace the discomfort and know expansion will come.

The best thing you can do is listen to yourself—with a healthy dose of self-awareness and a whole lot of love. Don't let others steer your ship. It's easy to allow others to influence you. It can be in small moments—like deciding where to eat for dinner—as well as big ones—like which job offer to accept. We doubt our own capabilities and our own knowing. With each doubt, our voice gets hidden—deeper and deeper until we can't hear it anymore. Finding yourself is about rediscovering your voice. Listening and turning within to see what you really want and then finding ways to express it in the outside world.

Consider something as simple as deciding where to eat for dinner. That may seem like a pretty simple question, but your default response may be: *It doesn't matter* or *I don't care*. You may not care all that much or don't want to cause a stir, so it's easier to go along with what the other person wants. If you multiply that by 365 days—that's a whole year of not caring what you eat for 1/3 of your meals. It may seem silly, but each of those responses is dimming your connection to your body—for feeling what you really want and denying your voice for expressing what you really want. Over time, this compounds enough that you lose your voice. You disconnect from your body and have trouble understanding what you even want. Now, amplify that to big changes and decisions in your life—jobs, moving, relationships, family, etc. If you don't know how to make decisions in small moments, how will you know what to decide in the big moments? We'll cover decision making in more detail in Part 6: Integration. For now, it's important to recognize and start paying more attention to yourself.

Activity 2.1

Creative Practices For Self-Expression

An important aspect of learning more about who you truly are is taking the time for self-expression. Many of us move through our days going to work, taking care of children or elderly parents, and moving through the motions to get through the day. I get it. I've done the same thing. There are times when we need to show up and get things done. However, the longer we do this without also taking care of ourselves and finding creative outlets for our self-expression, the more lost we can become in our own lives.

Do you have hobbies and creative activities you do for yourself because you enjoy them? We're often led to believe in adulthood that everything is about responsibilities and to do lists, however, this is not the case. Creative self-expression is an incredibly important part of being human and living this life. When we don't express ourselves in creative ways, chances are our feelings and emotions are being buried within our bodies. When we suppress these emotions, they get stuck and we begin to see the effects of it within our bodies in terms of ailments and illness. We'll cover more on this in Part 4: The Body. In the meantime, take this time to reflect on your relationship to creativity and self-expression with the activity below.

Do you allow yourself to express yourself creatively? Some creative activities may include: dancing, singing, drawing, playing an instrument, playing sports, gardening, journaling, sculpting, or photography.

_____

_____

_____

_____

_____

Do you share your emotions with others, or do you keep every-thing bottled up inside of you? If you don't take the time for creative self-expression, ask yourself why that might be and how you may start to shift that.

_____

_____

_____

_____

_____

_____

Reflection 2.3

Self-Expression

- What is your relationship with self-expression?

- Do you find it challenging to express yourself?

- What do you love to do even (and most especially) if there seems to be no point or end goal to it?

- Where do you spend time during the day doing something that you love to do?

_____

_____

_____

_____

_____

Part 2: Key Takeaways

The Whole Self

- What you desire is already within you.

- Self-responsibility is the act of taking responsibility for your own actions. It's about admitting the role you play in your life and recognizing that you have agency over your life.

- Taking care of your own mind and body are critical parts of strengthening your mind-body connection.

- Identify your fears and work to heal them.

- Embrace creative practices to support your self-discovery journey.

The 10 Most Important Things You Can Do for Your Whole Self

1. Love yourself deeply

2. Listen to your body

3. Speak your truth

4. Do things that bring you joy in all areas of life

5. Appreciate the little moments

6. Rewire your brain for more joy and less negativity

7. Express your emotions—with therapy, art, exercise, etc.

8. Take care of yourself for the long term (health, finances, etc.)

9. Spend time with people you love that make you feel seen, heard, and appreciated for who you are

10. Be YOU!

Additional Activities & Tools For The Whole Self

Activity 2.2

Self Check Ins

Daily self check-ins are a great way to stay in touch with how you are taking care of yourself. This can be done every morning when you wake up or every evening before bed. Take a few minutes to check in with yourself.

At the start of the day, I invite you to reflect on:

- What is your energy level at this moment?
- What is your intention for the day?

_____

_____

_____

_____

_____

At the end of the day, I invite you to reflect on:

- Did you pay attention to and manage your energy throughout the day?
- Did you stay present and connected to your intention for the day?

_____

_____

_____

_____

_____

Feel free to adapt these questions or replace them with other ones. The goal is to regularly check in with yourself. Remember, this work is all about finding what works for you.

Activity 2.3

Setting Intentions

Setting intentions can be a powerful way to move about the world in a way that allows you to stay connected to yourself and what you really want. Goals can be helpful to have as a target and it's important to continue to check in with your intentions.

I find this is a more flow-centered approach that allows me to stay in the moment and be more connected to who I am and where I want go (in broad terms). You'll see more of what I mean by this in Part 5: The Soul.

When we try to plan too much, it can take away from magical opportunities that we may not even be able to see or know for ourselves in this moment. I've seen it time and time again in my own life as well as with clients. Choosing how to move through the day creates more alignment and allows you to stay in the present moment more often. This allows you to watch beautiful opportunities unfold.

You can set intentions for life or business by brainstorming around your future self.

In this activity, feel into where you want to be in 6 months, 1 year, 3 years, or 5 years from now.

- What does your life look like?
- How are you living day to day?
- How are you of service in the world?
- How do you feel in your body?
- While you won't know exactly what you are 'doing', what are some of the things you'd like to see in your life?

_____

_____

_____

_____

_____

_____

_____

_____

_____

_____

_____

_____

_____

_____

_____

_____

_____

_____

_____

_____

_____

_____

_____

_____

_____

_____

_____

_____

_____

_____

_____

_____

_____

_____

_____

_____

_____

_____

_____

_____

_____

_____

_____

I invite you to journal or meditate on these prompts as a way to start the creativity process. Dream and feel into what you want. Don't be shy. If you're feeling sensitive about it, remember that no one has to even know about this activity except you. If you'd like to share your intentions with me, please feel free to email me at hello@maryclavieres.com or connect with me on social media.

List of Values

Adapted from Berkley Well-Being Institute.

- Acceptance
- Accomplishment
- Accountability
- Achievement
- Adaptability
- Adventurousness
- Agreeableness
- Alertness
- Altruism
- Ambition
- Amusement
- Art
- Assertiveness
- Authenticity
- Balance
- Beauty
- Being admirable
- Being dynamic
- Being earnest
- Being famous
- Being frank
- Being personable
- Being reasonable
- Being skilled
- Being thoughtful
- Being understanding
- Big-thinking
- Boldness
- Bravery
- Brilliance
- Calmness
- Capability
- Caring
- Cautiousness
- Certainty
- Challenge
- Charity
- Charm
- Cheerfulness
- Clarity
- Comfort
- Commitment
- Common sense
- Communication
- Community
- Compassion
- Confidence
- Connection
- Consideration
- Consistency
- Constructiveness
- Contemplation
- Contentment
- Contribution
- Control
- Conviction
- Cooperation
- Courage
- Creativity
- Credibility
- Curiosity

- Decency
- Decisiveness
- Democracy
- Dependability
- Determination
- Devotion
- Dignity
- Discipline
- Discovery
- Diversity
- Easygoingness
- Education
- Effectiveness
- Efficiency
- Elegance
- Emotional awareness
- Empathy
- Empowerment
- Energy
- Enjoyment
- Enthusiasm
- Equality
- Ethics
- Excellence
- Excitement
- Experimenting
- Exploration
- Expressiveness
- Fairness
- Faith
- Family
- Feelings
- Fidelity
- Flexibility
- Focus
- Forgiveness
- Freedom
- Freethinking
- Friendliness
- Friendship
- Fun
- Fun-loving attitude
- Generosity
- Gentleness
- Genuineness
- Good-nature
- Grace
- Gratitude
- Greatness
- Growth
- Happiness
- Hard work
- Harmony
- Health
- Helpfulness
- Honesty
- Honor
- Hope
- Humility
- Humor
- Grace

- Gratitude
- Greatness
- Growth
- Happiness
- Hard work
- Harmony
- Health
- Helpfulness
- Honesty
- Honor
- Hope
- Humility
- Humor
- Idealism
- Imagination
- Independence
- Individuality
- Influence
- Innovation
- Inspiration
- Integrity
- Intelligence
- Intuitiveness
- Joy
- Justice
- Kindness
- Knowledge
- Leadership
- Learning
- Life direction
- Life experience
- Logic
- Love
- Loyalty
- Mastery
- Maturity
- Moderation
- Modesty
- Motivation
- Neutrality
- Niceness
- Objectivity
- Open-mindedness
- Openness
- Optimism
- Organization
- Originality
- Passion
- Patience
- Peace
- Performance
- Persistence
- Playfulness
- Pleasure
- Positive attitude
- Positivity
- Potential
- Power
- Practicality
- Presence
- Principles

- Productivity
- Professionalism
- Prosperity
- Protection
- Punctuality
- Purpose
- Quality
- Recognition
- Recreation
- Reflection
- Relaxation
- Reliability
- Resourcefulness
- Respect for others
- Respect for self
- Responsibility
- Results-oriented
- Romance
- Satisfaction
- Security
- Self-awareness
- Self-improvement
- Self-reliance
- Self-respect
- Self-sufficiency
- Selflessness
- Satisfaction
- Security
- Self-awareness
- Self-improvement
- Self-reliance
- Self-respect
- Self-sufficiency
- Selflessness
- Serenity
- Service
- Simplicity
- Social connection
- Sophistication
- Spirituality
- Spontaneity
- Stability
- Steadiness
- Strength
- Structure
- Success
- Sympathy
- Teamwork
- Tenderness
- Tidiness
- Tolerance
- Tradition
- Transformation
- Trust
- Truth
- Variety
- Unity
- Warmth
- Wealth
- Well-roundedness
- Wisdom

Activity 2.4

What makes you, you?
Identifying your values.

An activity that is helpful for staying aligned with your intentions, as well as making it easier to make decisions, is identifying your values.

By having a set of values you can stand behind, it allows you to more easily see what may or may not be for you. Your values can serve as guideposts and aid in decision making.

For example: Let's say you have a strong value about the environment and supporting eco-friendly initiatives is important to you. You value and care about the Earth. If you get asked to apply for a job that is with an oil company, you may decide it's not something you want to pursue because it isn't aligned with your value of caring for and protecting the planet. That's not to say that oil companies don't have eco-friendly initiatives, but you may choose to work at a company that produces solar power panels over oil. In order to be able to make that decision or even know where it's coming from within you, having a defined set of values is an important part of that foundation.

1. Choose 20 or so words from the value list[1] without overthinking.
2. From there, choose your top 10 words.
3. What are the themes you see coming up within these words?
4. Identify your top 5-7 values that you want to prioritize and live by in your life.
5. Keep them listed in your office or around your house to remind you of them on a daily basis.
6. Refer to this list whenever you are faced with a decision or situation that you are unsure about.

_____

_____

_____

_____

_____

_____

_____

_____

_____

_____

_____

Tool 2.1

Journaling

The process of journaling can be very healing. I especially enjoy using *The Artist's Way Journal* by Julia Cameron.[1] The premise with this journal is to write three pages every morning. The invitation is to write down all the clutter and worries floating around in your brain. This process allows you to get them down on paper without judgment and without trying to change anything. When I first started journaling, it felt a little uncomfortable because I wasn't used to getting my thoughts down on paper in this way. However, once I got used to it and opened up, I couldn't stop writing. You can write about the highs, the lows, and anything in between. Your journal isn't something meant for anyone else except you. Embrace this safe space as a way to connect more deeply with yourself. You may be surprised as to what comes up.

Tips for journaling:

- Be open to writing without thought or judgment as to what you're putting on the page.

- Let your mind wander and write whatever comes
  to you.

- If it feels uncomfortable at first, sit with this
  discomfort and keep writing. You'll get used to it.

- The level of openness you write with will allow you to
  discover new depths within yourself.

Tool 2.2

Walks in Nature

There is a movement evolving around Eco Therapy, which is a modality that focuses on spending time in nature. Nature can be incredibly healing and I have found that to be true for myself. This activity allows you to take in the world around you—observe the plants and animals and watch the change of seasons. It is best that this time in nature is done without being on your phone and listening to audiobooks or podcasts. It's a time for you to connect more deeply to nature, which will, in turn, allow you to connect more deeply to yourself.

There are many healing benefits of being in nature. According to mind.org, these benefits include:

- improve your mood
- reduce feelings of stress or anger
- help you take time out and feel more relaxed
- improve your physical health
- improve your confidence and self-esteem
- help you be more active

- help you meet and get to know new people
- connect you to your local community
- reduce loneliness
- help you feel more connected to nature
- provide peer support.[1]

My walks in nature start as a way for me to take a small break from being in the house most of the day since I mainly work from home. It became such a comfort for me that my body started to crave that time and space.

List 1–3 moments throughout your day where you can fit in a walk, even if only for 5–10 minutes.

_____

_____

_____

_____

_____

_____

Tool 2.3

Meditation

Meditation is a tool that invites you to sit with yourself and clear your mind. A common misconception with meditation is people think it needs to be a long and intense process. It can feel intimidating for anyone just starting out, but it doesn't have to be this way. My dear friend, Elizabeth Guilbeault from Every Day Energy with Elizabeth, teaches us that meditation can be taking 1 minute to ground yourself in a busy environment or taking 5 minutes to sit quietly before your next task. Meditation doesn't have to be sitting in a dark room for 30 minutes in order for it to be effective. I'm a big believer in finding what works best for you —in all areas of your life. This includes how you approach meditation or other healing and connection modalities.

If you are trying meditation for the first time, I invite you to start with one of these options:

- Take 3 deep, full breaths and bring awareness to your feet on the ground.

- Spend a moment feeling your feet fully connected to the earth.
- Imagine the flow of energy between yourself and the earth as giving and receiving.
- Feel your connectedness and allow it to center and ground your body into a more relaxed, deeply knowing state.

OR

- Find a quiet space to sit or lie down for five minutes.
- Focus on the sound of your breath.
- If you get distracted and thoughts creep in, go back to focusing on your breath.
- You may find calm instrumental music supportive in this practice.

You can learn more about Elizabeth (and try out her fantastic meditations) at Every Day Energy with Elizabeth.

Reminder:

You are love.

Part 3:
The Mind

Understanding The Mind

Your mind is powerful. It controls your thoughts and beliefs, which impacts how you move about the world. Your mind has thoughts right now, even as you read this book. It might be about what you're learning. It could also be about what you're going to have for dinner or plans for the weekend. Your thoughts are always there. An important step in transformation is understanding what your thoughts are currently telling you and recognizing how they may be holding you back. Only then can you really change them to create something different for yourself.

I tell my daughters all the time that our minds can (and do!) play tricks on us. In fact, the mind is really good at that because its job is to keep us safe.

This isn't a bad thing, but it is good to stop and think: *What is my mind telling me?*

"In 2005, the National Science Foundation published an article regarding research about human thoughts per day. The average person has about 12,000 to 60,000 thoughts per day. Of those, 95% are exactly the same repetitive thoughts as the day before and about 80% are negative."[1]

Why is this important to know?

You are what you think.

We need to understand where our thoughts are coming from in order to reframe them into something different. Negative thoughts are especially limiting because they will keep you from seeing new possibilities. If you think about the fact that you have your own negative thoughts and add on the negative thoughts of the people you surround yourself with, that's a lot of negativity! It's natural and also important to be aware of.

Remember, if you continue to operate how you've always operated, you won't get different results.

What Holds You Back

Self, Meet Fear

B ecoming aware of your beliefs and understanding what you can control in your life are powerful ways to improve your mind-body connection to shift the trajectory of your life. Identifying your fears is another critical component of this work.

Are you someone that faces your fears or do you tend to shy away from them? You might consider yourself somewhere in between. While facing your fears is not easy and can take quite a few deep acts of courage, it's another way to have deeply transformational experiences in your life.

I used to shy away from some big fears. For most of my life, I had a debilitating fear of heights. While flying in airplanes wasn't an issue, many other things were, including climbing tall staircases, walking over bridges, riding ski lifts, and more. It was only around the start of my biggest transformational journey (which also started me on the path to writing this book) that I could face the fear of heights. Through an incredible sequence of events and experiences, I was able to overcome my fear of heights and ride in a hot-air balloon at sunrise over Luxor, Egypt.

I was once told the places we are meant to go in our lives are on the opposite side of our fears. After healing my fear of heights, I am able to see that in a whole new way. This experience drove me to explore other fears in my life and begin healing those parts of myself.

The first step is identifying the fear. This may seem pretty easy in a lot of cases, but not every case. I do believe some of our fears stem from generational wounds and experiences that happened in other lifetimes. My fear of heights is a good example. It is something I had since childhood, without any known reason or experience to go with it. I later found out through my dream space that I was thrown off a cliff in another lifetime. I believe that is at least part of where my fear originated.

After you identify the fear, the next step is being willing to work with it and begin the healing process. This is not done from the mind. Your mind may resist you taking on this work. It might feel scared of the unknown or too comfortable with how it's been operating. That's ok. As you commit to this path, you will pave the way for more healing to be done. Your fears and subsequent healing will need to be felt within the body to move through it. I'll cover more on that in Part 4: The Body.

Note: It's great to have a network of practitioners and healers that can support you in this work. Whether it is through trauma informed work or other modalities, please research credentials and get referrals before committing to working with someone.

Activity 3.1

Identifying Your Fears

I invite you to identify some of your biggest fears. They may be things that seem very obvious, like a fear of heights or fear of a specific animal / reptile / insect. They may also be fears that are a little harder to tangibly see, such as a fear of speaking in public or a fear of failure.

Ask yourself these questions:

- What are you most afraid of?
- Why are you afraid of it?
- What is your earliest memory of having this fear?
- Is there a specific incident in your life that brought this fear forward for you?

Take some time to journal and brainstorm around your fears. If nothing comes to mind right away, sit with this inquiry and over time, something may become clear to you. We all have fears of some sort and that's ok. It's part of the human experience. If you have a difficult time identifying your fears, your fears could be buried deep down as things that you don't want to face. That's ok. Healing comes to those who choose it when they are ready.

There is no right or wrong path for you to be on in this moment. If tackling your fears seems too challenging right now, you can always revisit this section of the book at a later time.

_____

_____

_____

_____

_____

_____

_____

_____

_____

_____

_____

_____

Mental Blocks

Mental blocks are another area where you may find yourself stuck. The mind always thinks it's serving its purpose and doing its job by keeping you safe. The growth and expansion come from recognizing when the mind is holding you back and working through it. Below are areas of mental blocks that I have seen with clients and also experienced myself. Take note of which ones resonate most with you as they may be good places for you to look deeper into for your own healing.

People Pleasing

We are typically shown from a young age that it's important to be mindful of our actions out of concern for what other people think. Whether it's out of maintaining a certain image or specific beliefs regarding manners and etiquette, we are often taught to worry about and put others first. That we should weigh the consequences of our actions by what other people will think. Constantly worrying about what others think won't get you anywhere. In fact, it will keep you stuck in big ways.

It's time to get rid of this mental block. If you worry about what everyone else will think, you'll never take one step on your own path. At the end of the day, it's your life that you're living—not someone else's.

Perfectionism

If you are waiting for things to be perfect before taking your next step, it's a surefire way to stay exactly where you are. Perfection is an unattainable expectation. It does not exist. Everything is perfectly imperfect as it is, so there is no higher achievement to work toward. When your mind wants you to have everything figured out and ensure an outcome can be reached in a certain way, it is telling you that it isn't safe to try new things or make mistakes.

Not allowing yourself to make mistakes is a pretty closed perspective to have if you have dreams you want to achieve. Instead of faulting yourself for your mistakes, recognize the lessons that lead you down new paths and give you new experiences.

If you struggle with perfectionism, you may have trouble recognizing when enough is enough. Determining when it's time to move on and make a change is a delicate balance of honoring your mind and listening to your body. Your mind may want to have everything exactly planned out, but your body will innately know when it feels ready. Don't let your mind hold you back. More to come on this in Part 4: The Body.

Imposter Syndrome

Have you ever thought that you aren't good enough at something to give it a try? You see others that are (seemingly) excelling in the area you want to be in and you think, *Who am I to think I can be there too?* It's normal to think this sometimes. Your mind is keeping you safe (again). When you allow yourself to stay in the space of not deserving to be where you want to be or thinking that you aren't good enough, you are stopping yourself in your tracks.

According to Merriam-Webster, "a psychological condition that is characterized by persistent doubt concerning one's abilities or accomplishments accompanied by the fear of being exposed as a fraud despite evidence of one's ongoing success."[1]

When imposter syndrome shows up, remind yourself of your accomplishments and how far you've come. Sometimes we need a little extra self-love and celebration to combat the doubt and insecurities that imposter syndrome brings up. The truth is, people that are more than qualified to be where they are, are the ones that suffer from imposter syndrome the most. People that are faking their way to the top don't usually worry about things like this—they just go for it. Remind yourself of that the next time you doubt your abilities and know that you deserve to be in the arena too.

Guilt

Guilt is another perspective that keeps many people stuck. As a mom, I relate to guilt on many levels. I feel guilty and worry that I'm not doing enough for my daughters and that time spent away from them makes me a bad mom. I know this isn't true and yet, I still feel guilt creep in. When that happens, I remind myself of the truth. The truth is, having time away from my daughters refuels and makes me a better mom. It allows me to be a stronger parent with more love, patience, and understanding for their own growth.

Knowing this doesn't stop the guilt from showing up in my

weak moments. The trick is to bring awareness to it, allow it to sit with me (all feelings are valid!), and move through it so that I can get back on track to being the healthiest version of myself for my daughters.

Comparison

It's easy to compare yourself to others as a way to keep yourself from moving forward. When you compare to someone else, you see what you don't have or what you lack in some way. When you tell yourself you are missing that one thing someone else has, it gives you a reason to stay where you are. It stops you in your tracks and prevents you from even trying.
Comparison can also be disguised as admiring what someone else has or where they are in their process. Remember, each and every one of us is on our own unique journey. You may find inspiration from people along the way, but be mindful of attaching to that and holding on to it as your own path.

Chasing the Next Level

When you want to be further along, you are focusing on the lack and what you don't have in this moment. There is nothing inherently wrong with wanting to be somewhere else. Many of us have goals and dreams we hope to live out in this lifetime. When you are focused on what you don't have, you are living in a low expression of your potential. In your high expression, you will be connected and understand that where you are now is exactly where you need to be. With a gratitude practice and acceptance of where you are, you will continue to solidify your foundation and build upon it in a new way. Over time, you will see where you wanted to be is unfolding for you in the now.

The Truth Is . . .

When you find yourself with a negative or pessimistic viewpoint, your mind is likely being extra critical of your situation. If you're anything like me, your first inclination is to jump to the worst-case scenario. This is you being too hard on yourself.

If this is the case, this activity is an invitation to take a look at the full situation, including the best-case scenario. Try completing this statement:

The truth is . . .

Repeat this statement and complete it with other thoughts. This statement will help your mind to find other possibilities within your current circumstances—likely ones that aren't as dire.

For example, if I am being hard on myself about not accomplishing XYZ or being behind on something, instead of berating myself and telling myself that I never finish anything, I can use this statement.

The truth is . . . I did accomplish something, it was just different from what I planned.

The truth is . . . a different priority came up that I worked on instead.

The truth is . . . I didn't allocate enough time to complete XYZ. Now I know where I can improve for next time.

Do you see the difference? Instead of staying in the negative of something you didn't do, you can pull yourself back to look at the full situation and see other areas that highlight something positive.

Activity 3.2

The Truth Is . . .

Identify a story you've been telling yourself that keeps you stuck in a spiral of negativity, self-doubt, or another mental block. Use that situation to complete the sentence "The truth is . . . "

Identify what's really true about the situation and reprogram the way you see that situation from a place of empowerment.

_____

_____

_____

_____

_____

_____

Creating A New Reality

Shaping Your Experience

We all carry beliefs about the world around us. Once we have these beliefs and hold on to them, they start to dictate our thoughts and our actions. Beliefs also color our perspective in the world and are the starting point of our judgments. Everything filters through our beliefs. *Everything*.

Have you ever heard the expression *money doesn't grow on trees*? Chances are you heard it as a child and it stayed with you. This expression is meant to convey that money is not easy to obtain or have in some way. It's not as simple as the leaves that grow on trees.

The thing is, this expression is a belief. It's a belief that money is hard to obtain. But is that the truth? It is A truth, but it doesn't have to be YOUR truth. Personally, I'd rather believe that money is easy to obtain, that it's something I can expect to be around and all I have to do is think about money for it to appear. This is simply one phrase and one belief. We all have thousands of them in our heads. This isn't meant to stress you out and worry about all your beliefs. It's simply an invitation to get curious about them so you can shift any negative or non-empowering beliefs to stronger, more empowering ones.

If you'd like to dig deeper into money beliefs, I highly recommend the book *Think and Grow Rich* by Napoleon Hill (the unabridged version). He studied the wealthiest people of his time for over 25 years and compiled the key traits he believed all of them had in order to become rich. For a modern take on money mindset, I highly recommend *You Are a Badass at Making Money* by Jen Sincero.

True transformation and everlasting change require you to examine all of your beliefs. To really take a look at them and determine what is your truth or not. It can feel scary to realize that the beliefs you've grown up with may not be the ones that hold true to you today. As you examine them and challenge your personal status quo, you will realize there is a completely different way to look at your life. One that comes from a place of strength, trust, love, and deeper understanding of the world around you.

Before we dive deeper into the programming of the mind, let's level set with a few definitions.

Belief: an acceptance that something exists or is true, especially one without proof; trust, faith, or confidence in (someone or something).[1]

Thought: an idea or opinion produced by thinking, or occurring suddenly in the mind.[2]

Perspective: a particular attitude toward or way of regarding something; a point of view.[3]

Judgment: an opinion or conclusion likely without facts or overtaken by emotion.[4]

Getting a Different Result in Your Life

It is well known that the results you achieve are created by the actions you take. What most don't realize is that your experiences and beliefs are driving those actions. A great tool to express this principle is The Results Pyramid®, created by Roger Conners and Tom Smith[5]. The Results Pyramid® explains that your end results are originally shaped by your experiences. A specific experience or interaction that you have creates a belief about something. You then use that belief to decide what you take action on and what you don't. Those actions then drive the results you see in your life.

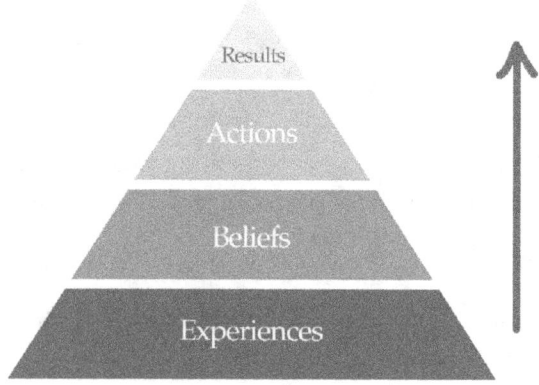

As an example, if I go to a gym class and find it's too hard and I don't enjoy it (experience), then I might think I'm not cut out for exercise (belief). That would then cause me to not go back to a gym class (action) and I wouldn't achieve my goal whether it was to become more flexible, lose weight, gain strength, etc. (result).

On the other hand, if I went to the gym with a friend and we supported each other through the workout (experience), I might think working out is fun and easy (belief). This would make me excited to go back to the gym (action) and I could more easily reach my goal (result).

Do you see the difference? Creating experiences that are supportive of your desired outcomes is an important part of making lasting change.

Sometimes it can be pretty clear what the experience is that is driving us, like in the gym example earlier. Other times, it may be harder to see—potentially something from our childhood we've blocked out. We typically have a lot of old experiences and beliefs about money, food, work, etc. that stay with us into adulthood. Hearing these points of view can then shape your life in a way you may not even recognize. This is part of why it's important to look at the thoughts that come up for you; to know what your brain is telling you so you can reprogram it with something different.

There may also be times where an experience stays with you, but you don't see it come together in a specific way in that moment. About 15 years ago, I remember walking down the hallway of my corporate job when a voice came to me and said, *Is this all there is?* It felt like a whisper in my mind, yet it was also clear as day. The deep question took me by surprise. While I didn't have a specific answer to it in the moment, that experience stayed with me. It gave me permission to look at my life differently and question my path. Eventually, it led to me taking steps to start a product business. From there, a completely new path opened up. I left my corporate job to become a business owner full time. I now work with individuals and companies that want to make big changes and transformations. Whether it's through Executive Advisory, Business Coaching, or Human Design readings, I support individuals with connecting more deeply with their mind-body connection. Becoming a business owner isn't for everyone, but in following my path and the whispers of my heart, it was the best decision for me.

Knowing You Always Have a Choice

Did you know that you have a choice in every moment? You can choose your actions and also choose your thoughts. You can choose if you want to respond to something in anger or if you want to respond to it with love and acceptance.

This can feel like a hard concept to grasp because most of the time, it's easier to get caught up in emotions and blame other people or other circumstances. It's easier to tell yourself that you don't have a choice because of XYZ. Not that there is always one great option and one not great option within your choices. You still may not like both choices in a given situation, but there is always a choice.

This can often show up in relationships. If there is a case of hurt or resentment, it is easy to hold on to that feeling. However, you still have a choice. You can choose to move on to a path of taking the higher road or even forgiveness. That doesn't mean it feels easy to do. In fact, it's probably the harder choice. Most people hold on to resentment because it's easier. I've certainly done that in different parts of my life. It's only when you recognize the only person you're hurting by holding on to those feeling is yourself, that you can see things differently.

Note: The types of choices I am speaking about here are coming from an incredibly privileged place. There are many people hurting in the world that are not given the same freedom and choices as white heterosexuals. Many communities, including Black, Brown, Indigenous, and LBGTQIA+ fear for their safety based on choices of the White population. This is most certainly not supportive to humanity or coming from a place of love. This perspective on choice is not meant to belittle or harm those mentioned.

Recognizing What You Can Control

People underestimate how much control they have when it comes to their own life. Sometimes it's easier to blame others and play the victim. You may not even be aware of the patterns while you're in them—especially if they are patterns that started in childhood. And while yes, other people's actions can impact you, you still have a choice in how you react and what you control.

Here is an example. One thing most of us can probably agree on is that we can't control the weather. Ever changing and unpredictable, it makes it a challenge to know what will happen next. However, there is something we can control about the weather: How we prepare for it. If we think it might rain, we can pack an umbrella. Being prepared can then change how we react. Instead of getting soaked and frustrated that we're wet, we can pull out an umbrella and stay comfortable in a wet situation. Being comfortable may prevent us from getting frustrated with the rain.

Making choices for yourself gives you agency over your life and this is what you can control.

Letting Go of Expectations

A friend and teacher of mine, Jamie Palmer, once said, *"Expectations are the root of our suffering."* It hit me hard and resonated deeply when I heard her say this.

I've always found expectations to be tricky. On the one hand, if you look at expectations more like goals related to something you want to happen, they can help you stay inspired and passionate about your future. On the other hand, if you get too attached, you end up having your goals in a grip and can't let go, which usually ends in disappointment. When that happens, you don't allow space for new possibilities. The universe is almost always working to give you something better than you can imagine, but if you hold your goals tight, it doesn't give you room for those options to come to life.

Early on in my coaching business, I'd get frustrated if a potential client came to me asking questions about something I thought I'd been clear about or if someone said they were going to sign up for a service and didn't follow through. I soon realized I was coming to the table with a whole list of expectations of what I thought others *should* do. Needless to say, this is not a healthy place to work from and not supportive for anyone involved. It wasn't the energy I wanted to show up with, so I decided to let go of expectations and lean into trust. I cannot control or predict what others do or don't do, so why was I worrying about it?

The universe can deliver our dreams in an infinite number of ways and is typically better than what we can imagine. When we add expectations of what we *think* an outcome *should* look like, it prevents the universe from using all available resources to deliver on our desires. It doesn't leave room for your dreams to come to life in the best way possible.

Periodically check in with yourself and ask if you are holding on to your dreams too tightly. Releasing your grip is a way to stay present and invite in other possibilities. When you allow your mind's worrying to take a back seat and embody the belief that you know it will all work out, the expectations will fade away and you will be guided by your inner knowing.

The Power of Gratitude

As explained via The Results Pyramid®, your inner thoughts and beliefs deeply shape how you move about the world. This also impacts how you see the world. Take a look at your surroundings. Most likely, there are things you'd like to change about them. The truth is, your inner thoughts are what shape your outside world.

Gratitude is a powerful way to shift your mind and focus on

positive reinforcement. A lot of people may be quick to dismiss the power of gratitude, but this is the perfect place to start. Recognizing what you already have goes a long way toward arriving at a peace with yourself while also working toward a goal or dream.

By paying attention to what you are grateful for, you will retrain your brain to focus on what you have (abundance) instead of what you feel is missing in your life (lack). The feeling of gratitude and a recognition gives you a positive foundation to build from, allowing for expansion and growth.

When you focus on what you're grateful for and how much you appreciate things in your life, your world becomes so much bigger, brighter, and fuller.

There are many parts of our day to day lives that we take for granted because we get used to them. We get so used to them that we don't even give them a thought.

As an everyday example, my family moved to France a few years ago and we don't have air conditioning here. I have a bigger appreciation for air conditioning now than I had in the US. My body was so used to having it that I had to adjust to not having it. Air conditioning in the peak of summer heat is now something I don't take for granted.

Gratitude can be for very material things like air conditioning or other comforts that you're used to having, such as electricity, running water, etc. Gratitude can also be things about ourselves and our bodies. How much do we take for granted our fingers, our toes, and everything that allows our body to function each of our organs? My guess is we take all of that for granted 99% of the time.

I went to a yoga class, and we spent part of the time focusing on each body part. We had to zero in on every part and give thanks to it. Whether it was the lungs, intestines, or the heart, we were invited to notice all the different parts that make up our body and allow us to be in this form that we're in right now. It's really incredible when you think about it.

Below are a few prompts to reflect on:

- What are 50 things you're grateful for?
- Are you taking time to recognize these things throughout your day?
- What is a talent or skill that you are grateful to have?
- Who is one person you are grateful to have in your life?

_____

_____

_____

_____

_____

_____

_____

_____

_____

_____

_____

_____

You may find over time, the more you are grateful for what you have around you, the more it will help to keep you grounded. It doesn't eliminate stress, overwhelm, or anxiety, but it does allow you to be more centered and calmer. It tends to put things in perspective for your life. A lot of what we can see and practice in terms of abundance and recognizing what we have starts with having gratitude.

There are many ways you can incorporate gratitude into your life. I recommend the Five Minute Journal® to my clients, which has you list out 3 things that you're grateful for each day. Sharing what you're grateful for over a meal with loved ones is another fun way to incorporate more gratitude into your life.

Even taking 1 minute a day to walk and call out all the things you're grateful for is a great way to get started. Everyone has 1 minute a day and this practice can change your life. It truly changed mine.

Find ways to dig deep, look inside, and ask yourself what are you grateful for. Allow yourself to get curious about it and invite gratitude into your everyday life. You'll be able to look at things with a new wonderment to it.

Activity 3.3

Build Your Gratitude Practice

An activity I love to do to start clients on reshaping their inner world is introducing a gratitude practice. Below are a few activities you can choose from to start your gratitude practice.

1. You can make your gratitude very simple so the habit is easier to keep up with:

- Put a notebook next to your bed.
- Every morning when you wake up, list 3 things you are grateful for.
- You can repeat the practice every evening by listing 3 things you are grateful for that happened that day.

2. Share what you are grateful for every evening at the dinner table.

3. Take a walk for 1 minute a day. During that minute, identify all of the things you are grateful for. Say them out loud. Feel the gratitude for them in your body.

4. If you prefer to be guided, the Five Minute Journal® by Intelligent Change is a great place to get started. For some people, it's easier to incorporate structure by using something that already exists. The important thing is to get started—in whatever way works best for you.

Part 3: Key Takeaways

The Mind

- Your experiences and beliefs shape your reality.

- Your mind is always trying to keep you safe. Learn to discern when this is warranted and when it's holding you back from your next level of growth.

- We all have mental blocks that hold us back. The most important thing is to keep showing up for yourself and working through those blocks.

- There are multiple choices and multiple perspectives to any given situation.

- Choose gratitude regularly.

Additional Activities & Tools For The Mind

Activity 3.4

What is your mind telling you?

When you take a deeper look at what your mind is telling you, you'll be able to transform your negative thoughts and rewire yourself for more success.

Step 1: List all the reasons you don't think you can reach the dream you have or why you haven't reached it yet.

It doesn't matter what the reasons are. Write them all down. It might be things like . . . it's too expensive, I don't have time, who am I to have <insert dream here>, I have other commitments, etc. List all of them. Every single reason.

_____

_____

_____

_____

_____

_____

_____

_____

_____

Step 2: Take a look at your list and notice any patterns you see. What comes up most? Is it a lack of time, is it a lack of belief in yourself, or something else?

When you can identify patterns and see where the mind tries to keep you safe, it makes it easier to move through it. Identifying your patterns and bringing them into your awareness are the first steps to making a bigger change in your life.

_____

_____

_____

_____

_____

_____

_____

Step 3: Choose one of these reasons / patterns to work through.

How can you change your pattern for something more supportive to you?

For example, if you doubt yourself and your abilities, you can create a mantra to replace the doubt. Any time you find yourself saying. *I can't do this* or *I don't know what I'm doing,* replace it with, *I've got this. I know what I'm doing* or *I may not know the answer right now, but I'm figuring it out.*

Choose something empowering to tell yourself, then every single time you catch your mind telling you an old pattern, replace it with your new mantra. It may take time in the beginning, but it really works. Stick with it and it will become your new reality.

_____

_____

_____

_____

_____

_____

_____

_____

Activity 3.5

Reframing Your Mistakes

Do you often dwell on mistakes from your past? Reframing your mistakes is a great way to move forward and focus on the positive aspects of your life. Remember, what you think about expands. It's your choice what you focus on.

In this activity, you're invited to reframe your mistakes into lessons that have supported your growth. You can do this by taking a look at past 'mistakes' and exploring the lessons that have come from them.

Reflect on the following:

What are some experiences from your life that you view as mistakes in some way?

_____

_____

_____

_____

_____

_____

What good came from these 'mistakes'?

_____

_____

_____

_____

_____

How are you able to use the information you
learned for future projects or experiences?

_____

_____

_____

_____

_____

Tool 3.1

Affirmations

Affirmations are a great way to practice shifting your mindset and getting into higher alignment with yourself. You can make a list of statements you repeat to yourself daily (multiple times a day is even better). It may be hard to believe the affirmations at first, but over time, they will become a bigger part of your reality.

Something important to note is that as you practice the affirmations, also practice feeling the affirmation as a belief. To really change your reality isn't only about saying the affirmation, it's about practicing and saying it with feeling. Studies have shown that feeling the thought / affirmation is just as important (if not more) than simply saying it.

Examples of affirmations you can try:

- I love myself.
- I am grateful for this life.
- I am perfect as I am.
- I am abundant.

- I am open to the unknown.
- I am brave.
- I am creative.
- I am in flow.
- I am love.

If any of these affirmations feel difficult to say, check in with yourself to see if you have any underlying limiting beliefs that you'd like to work on. Also, feel free to create your own affirmations or add to this list.

Reminder:

Your mind is powerful. Choose your thoughts wisely.

Part 4:
The Body

Understanding The Body

Your body is powerful. While it holds all of your bones, organs, and blood flow to keep you alive and operating on Earth, it also hosts your deepest inner wisdom. It is speaking to you ALL THE TIME, whether you realize it or not. When you pay attention to this wisdom, you become more in control of your life. You stop your mind from running the show and get connected to more of who you really are. From there, you will be able to feel even more in alignment with your true self.

A large part of society is tuning into their bodies less, not more. You might see small groups of people paying attention to their bodies more, especially in holistically leaning circles, but a large majority of people on the planet are not in tune with their bodies. Just as they let their mind run the show with old, negative thought patterns and beliefs, they do something similar with their bodies. They tune out and don't pay attention to them. They only take notice when something is 'broken' or not working instead of listening on a continual basis. And even then, when they pay attention, it is usually to treat a symptom, not to get to the root cause and heal it. I call this a reactive approach to well-being instead of a proactive one.

Most people take their bodies for granted. They overload them with foods, drinks, and even medicines that are not serving them as a way to treat whatever pain it is they are experiencing. Please know that this isn't to debate whether medicine is good or bad for you. Like everything else, there is a time and place for it. What I'd like you to pay attention to is using these things in excess or as a way to numb the pain you are afraid to look at. I have been guilty of doing this and now work more consciously and more proactively with my body.

Just as we have different types of environments we thrive in, our bodies are all different. What might work for one body type might not work for another. Think about the way you eat or exercise compared to someone else you know. There are endless options out there, and it's up to you to find out what works for you. I've learned a lot about this through body exercises, human design, and studying differences in people and energy centers.

Along with food, you also store memories and emotions in your body. This can include joyful experiences as well as traumatic ones. These memories get stored in your body. If you don't consciously work on releasing them, over time, they will pile up and show up as fears, chronic illnesses, and even disease.

Remember my emergency dental visit from earlier? It was caused by my body feeling stressed and then (unknowingly) grinding my teeth at night. I ended up having to get a mouthguard to prevent more pain, and I wore it for many years. Only in the last couple of years was I able to stop using it. I attribute that to the time I've put into bodywork and somatic exercises to release stress and built up emotions. Anytime you can heal your body from something that is causing you pain, a powerful shift can occur that you'll be able to notice in other areas of your life.

If you have places in your body where you've experienced chronic pain, you may want to implement a body practice to begin to release whatever is stored there. I'm not a doctor and this is not medical advice. This is an invitation to look deeper into your relationship with your body. There may be things you want to explore or be open to in order to release stuck energy and heal your body. Remember, you're reading this with an open mind and a willingness to hear different perspectives, so if you feel called out, this is a great area to explore in more detail.

The Mind-Body Relationship

Our bodies are incredibly intuitive. They have survival instincts that allow us to respond to dangerous situations. Those same parts of our intuition are also trying to speak with us to guide us on our life path. Over time, we became disconnected from these instincts and stopped listening to our bodies.

You may try to ignore your thoughts and feelings, especially if you don't want to face them. Let's be honest, some thoughts and feelings are a lot to handle. They can be scary and confronting. I've ignored my fair share of feelings. As I quieted my voice over the years (i.e. didn't speak up or allow myself to be seen), I also blocked out things that didn't feel good, which suppressed my feelings, and then the symptoms started to show up in my body.

As you're looking to transform and lead your life in the way you want to lead it, you're going to want to use tools to quiet your mind. The mind is always there, so working with the body is a version of quieting the mind. It's about getting out of your mind and getting into your body. Your body knows so much.

That is the part of you that you want to be directing and deciding for you. When you can feel into a situation, you want to make a decision based on what your body is telling you, not based on your mind. The mind will try to act in ways that keep you safe, but it may also tell you things that aren't true in order to keep you safe. Your body will show you feelings that are aligned to your gut instincts and your true self. The goal is to pay attention to your body and allow that to guide you instead of your mind. Your body's wisdom is what's really connecting to you at a cellular level.

The first part is paying attention to your thoughts, paying attention to your mind, and recognizing what that is saying. As you start to observe and get a handle on it, you want to replace as many of those mind thoughts as you can, and then you want to get into your body. Let your innate being and the pure energy from your body wisdom come through instead of your mind.

The Physical Body

Listening and Speaking to Your Body

I n Part 2: The Whole Self, we spoke about some of the practical aspects of taking care of your physical body, including getting sleep, eating nourishing foods, and moving your body regularly. Another form of nourishment and caring for your physical body is listening and speaking to it.

Your body is speaking to you all the time.

Do you listen to it?
What is it telling you?
How often do you speak back to it?

Paying attention to how you feel in the moment and listening to what your body needs is an important part of deepening your mind-body connection. For example, if you feel a cramp in your leg, it would be best to get up and stretch—not ignore it and hope it will go away. This may seem like a pretty simple example, however, you might be surprised how often I encounter this with clients. Many people completely ignore taking breaks because they want to finish *one more thing*.

If you treat your body like the living, breathing thing it is, you may have an easier time taking care of it.

Start tuning in to see how your body is feeling at any given moment. As you listen more deeply and understand what it needs, you can respond to it more consciously. Speaking to your body regularly will build a deeper relationship with it. Similar to affirmations for your mind, you can also say affirmations to your body.

You can say things like . . .

I love you, my body.
Thank you for being strong.
Thank you for taking care of me.
You are strong and healthy.

Anything you feel called to say to show appreciation for this incredible body that shows up for you every day is something that can support your overall health.

Even if you are navigating chronic pain, speaking to your body can be a form of healing. It may not take away all the pain, but it can certainly support your mindset and impact your healing journey. I've had times in my life that I dealt with various body pains. Whenever I remembered to speak to my body lovingly, it shifted my mindset to move through the pain and healing differently. The truth is, your body is a magnificent form that performs incredible tasks every single day without you giving it much thought—the beat of your heart, the blood pumping through your veins, the digestive system processing food, and the brain directing the body to walk and talk, to name a few.

If this seems too much of a stretch for you, you can also think of the alternative and speak negatively to it (not recommended, of course). Whatever you think about expands, so if you say negative things to your body, your body will ingest that as its 'nourishment' instead of gratitude.

Activity 4.1

Speaking To Your Body

You're invited to start speaking to your body as if it is your best friend. Whenever you feel pain in your physical body, you can:

- Breathe into it and observe the pain.

- Ask your body what it is trying to tell you.

- Speak kindly. Tell your body what you love about it.

- Reassure your body that you will get through this pain.

- Ask your body to release any energies, emotions, or feelings it is holding on to.

Remind your body that as you develop this new area in your relationship (honoring it and paying attention to it), you will not need to feel pain as a way for it to speak to you. You will begin to pay attention to earlier signals, trust yourself, and navigate your choices differently.

As you get curious, allow yourself to stay open to releasing fears or stuck energy. Know that your body is taking care of you the best it knows how to. Embrace and trust in this next version of your relationship with your body.

The Energy Body

E verything is energy. Along with your physical body, you also have an Energy Body. Making sure your energy is flowing correctly throughout your body and not stuck is an important part of opening your mind-body connection. I love body tapping for exactly this reason. When you can get out of your mind and into your body, you're able to pinpoint areas you need to release stored and stuck energy to realign your system.

I am someone who has historically gotten headaches and the occasional migraine. When I started regularly doing body tapping exercises, the intensity and frequency of my headaches decreased. They didn't go away completely, but as I managed my anxious thoughts and also got out of my head and into my body, my energy completely shifted. I also used acupressure points to release blockages in parts of my face and hands that are known to be linked to headaches. When you experience pain somewhere in your body (especially recurring pain), it likely has an energetic component to it, along with the physical compo-nent. It's important to check in with your body and see how you can realign your energy to get yourself in a flow state again.

The Chakra System

This energy body has multiple layers that make up your aura along with your energy centers, also known as Chakras.

"Chakras are energy vortexes that exist within each of us. These energy vortexes transport energy from the universe around you into your aura and body, as well as between the physical body and the layers of your aura. You can think of your chakra system as similar to your spiritual bloodstream. Blood carries oxygen, nutrients, and hormones throughout the body; helps regulate and balance the body; and protects the body by removing waste products and clotting when the body is harmed. Much in the same way your bloodstream connects and supports your many other physical bodily systems, your chakra system connects and supports your physical self and your energy self." [1]

Below is a breakdown of the seven main chakras in the body.

THE CHAKRA SYSTEM

Crown Chakra

Thrid Eye Chakra

Throat Chakra

Heart Chakra

Solar Plexus Chakra

Sacral Chakra

Root Chakra

1st Root Chakra: I am (family of origin, overall well-being, stability, comfort)

2nd Sacral Chakra: I feel (gut feelings, sensuality, pleasure)

3rd Solar Plexus Chakra: I do (productivity, getting things done, strength, power)

4th Heart Chakra: I love (affinity for self and others, love / hate, acceptance)

5th Throat Chakra: I talk (communication with self and others, expression, creativity, inspiration)

6th Third Eye Chakra: I see (clairvoyance—ability to see clearly, intuition, meditation, trust)

7th Crown Chakra: I know (truth, connection to the god of your heart, knowledge, consciousness)

Spending time with and saying hello to reach of the chakras in your body is a great way to bring more awareness to your energy body on a regular basis.

Energy Management

Another part of making sure your energy is flowing correctly is managing your energy. When you don't pay attention to your energy and you let your mind run the show, it can lead to decision fatigue, burnout, and exhaustion. I see this often with my clients and used to operate like this myself. Whether it is not wanting to miss out, not wanting to say no, or truly enjoying all the different plans, it will eventually feel stressful running from one thing to the next and you'll end up exhausted afterward.

A mentor of mine, Pat Windom, introduced me to the concept

of energy dollars. It is a simple way to keep your energy top of mind. Look at your energy in terms of dollars. For example, you are allotted 100 energy dollars in any given day. Once you spend those dollars, you are running on empty. You need to be able to replenish your supply before continuing with activities. Different activities cost you different amounts of energy dollars (i.e. exercising vs visiting a friend vs attending an event, etc.). As you do different activities, pay attention to how much energy you are spending, along with how you feel afterward. Then you'll be able to average out the various events to see what is possible for you within a day without overdoing it. You can refine things over time. The first part is to get started and pay attention to your energy, how you feel throughout the day, and when you hit pressure points (meaning, you overspent your energy).

You can also replenish your energy dollars during the day by doing activities that refuel you. I love to take walks. This is part of what connects me to nature and grounds my being. After a walk, I always feel refreshed and in a positive mindset to move about the rest of my day. Find the things that work for you so you can replenish your energy when needed.

While sleep is most directly related to the physical body, it has a big impact on your energy body. The biggest and best way to replenish your energy is by having proper sleep. It's often overlooked, but sleep is vital for your mind and body. Studies show the impact poor sleep can have on the body, including our memory and attention, which can lead to slower, less accurate decision making. Poor sleep also impacts our emotions and can lead to depression and anxiety.[2] I cover more on decision making with energetics and your mind-body connection in my How to Make Better Decisions in Life and Business Workshop.[3]

The Emotional Body

A lot of us grow up thinking emotions are a bad thing because we've been taught not to express them. While women are told to be less emotional, men are taught to hide their emotions in order to be seen as 'tough'. Neither of these are helpful beliefs to accept or hold on to.

Most of this demand for emotional suppression is due to a majority of people (mainly the louder voices in society) not being comfortable with emotions or knowing how to handle them. What we have now is a world that is disconnected from their bodies and from their emotions. People are letting their mind run the show. When the mind runs the show, it usually makes choices out of fear because it wants to keep us safe. You can probably start to see how this can cause chaos with our emotions.

When we suppress our emotions, they stay stuck in our bodies. Eventually, they become so stuck and repressed health challenges manifest in our bodies. Harboring stress, for example, has been known to show symptoms in the body. Remember my jaw pain from earlier? This is a classic example of misalignment that caused pain to show up in the body. When I still had my corporate job, but was so miserable I wanted to leave, I started to have intense pain in my mouth and jaw to the point that I needed to go to the dentist. At the time, I hadn't been mindful of my own well-being (definitely not to the extent I am now) and I wasn't aware of the power of the mind-body connection. This experience with my mouth pain was probably one of my earliest wake-up calls to the work I do now.

Being able to heal yourself, regulate your emotions, and work with them takes deep work and dedication that most people are not willing to do. I do believe this is shifting as more people commit to their healing.

Emotional Guidance System (EGS)

Everyone has an Emotional Guidance System (EGS). Think of it as a GPS, but instead of giving you directions for driving, it is giving you alerts about your emotions. Feelings of joy and excitement show you're on the right track and moving toward more alignment. Feelings of heightened negative emotions (anger, stress, worry, frustration, bitterness, etc.) are your EGS showing you where there is more healing to be done.

As children, we have natural inclinations to be who we really are and to have our emotions on full display. It's one of the big ways we process energy in the moment. However, when we learn about the world around us, we may start to hide our emotions in order to fit in. I grew up as a very sensitive child that learned to hide and suppress my emotions over time. Worried about what others would think and not wanting to stand out from the crowd, it became my go to reaction to suppress my emotions. What I've come to learn is that suppressing emotions has so many negative side effects on the rest of your life. It can cause chronic stress and anxiety as well as losing connection to your true self.

Every time you can meet your emotions, especially pain or

discomfort, and move through it instead of ignoring it, lashing out, or burying it, is a progress step in your healing journey. Get curious about why your EGS is on alert. Where is the deeper pain? How can you forgive yourself and others to heal it? If your pain is very deep and related to trauma, please consider getting a licensed professional to work with you.

It's been many years of me learning to rediscover myself, honor my feelings, and rebuild my own self trust. This process has allowed me to reconnect with Little Mary (my name for my younger self) and embrace my true nature, which brings deeper meaning and purpose in new and exciting ways.

Your EGS is your free internal system, giving you a signal of what is not in alignment. Honor it and use it wisely.

Modalities to Connect to Your Body and Release Stored Emotions

We need to be able to express our emotions and move through them. If we can't do that, we will stay blocked from our connection to our soul. Below are modalities to connect to your body as a way to release stored emotions.

Body Tapping

Body tapping is one of my favorite ways to connect to my body and release stored emotions. It is a simple yet profound way to get out of your own way and heal yourself. As with anything new, it can feel strange when you first start out, but you get used to it.

A simple exercise to start with is called *Dahn Jon Tapping*. Take a relaxed stance with your legs shoulder-width apart. Your arms and legs should be relaxed and bent. Make fists with both of your hands. Place your hands about two inches below your belly button (on your Dahn Jon). Begin to alternate your hands and tap gently on your Dahn Jon. As you get comfortable with the movement, increase the speed of your tapping until you get to a place where you feel some discomfort, but not pain. Remember to breathe in and out and find a rhythm that works for you. When you're first starting out, you can try this for 3-5 minutes at a time and slowly work your way up to 10 or even 20 minutes. The longer or more intense the session, the more likely you will be able to stop your thinking brain and get into a flow state in your body.

You can also watch a video about this here:

Yoga

Yoga is a great combination of exercise, stretching, finding balance, and also connecting to your body. I love the simple yet effective practices from Yoga with Adriene on YouTube. You can start with very simple poses to work on your balance and work your way up to more advance strengthening exercises. Doing a morning yoga routine right after you wake up (even for 5-10 minutes) can be a great way to stretch and awaken your body for the day. When you find poses you enjoy, you can even take breaks from your work and do a few poses. It serves as a brain break and a stretch!

Breathwork

Breathwork is another tool I recommend to clients for connecting to the body. Whenever you intentionally manipulate your breath in this way, it alters the way your brain processes and calms your nervous system.

A simple breathing technique you can start with is Box Breathing.

Box Breathing in Four Steps:

- **Step 1:** Breathe in, counting to four slowly. Feel the air enter your lungs.
- **Step 2:** Hold your breath for 4 seconds. Try to avoid inhaling or exhaling for 4 seconds.
- **Step 3:** Slowly exhale through your mouth for 4 seconds.
- **Step 4:** Wait for another 4 seconds before you breathe in again.

Repeat this exercise as many times as you can. Thirty seconds of deep breathing will help you feel more relaxed and in control. [1]

Meditation

You may already be aware of meditation as a form of connecting to your body. I often find when I start working with clients that most people avoid it because they are too nervous to sit with their thoughts. If you feel this way, you can start with one of the other techniques mentioned above. If you have a busy mind, it may be easier to start with Body Tapping, Yoga, or Breathwork before sitting in stillness to meditate.
There are many ways you can meditate.

You can listen to a guided meditation where someone speaks to you and takes you through steps to check in with yourself.

You can sit quietly and listen to calming music. Music can be a little trickier to work with because you'll need to find something that allows you to tune everything else out. If the beat or rhythm changes too much, it might be distracting to use during meditation versus helpful. I personally like music that is slow and doesn't have many words, if any. Usually the words are a chant or in a different language, so I don't get distracted by the lyrics. Always remember to find what works for you.

You can do a body scan to check in with the different parts of your body and feel into them. This keeps you focused on your mind-body connection.

Scan the QR code below to download free meditations.

Activity 4.2

Getting Into Your Body

If your mind wants to overthink everything in a million different ways, bodywork can be a powerful practice. Some great tools for getting out of your mind and into your body are:

- Body Tapping

- Yoga (I love Yoga with Adriene on YouTube)

- Meditation

- Breathwork

- Walking in nature

These activities help you change your state and flip a switch in your brain to get some of that to quiet down so you can really hear and feel into your true self.

Choose an activity that feels interesting to you and start practicing it daily. (Even 5 minutes a day will be beneficial.)

A New Way Of Being

Neutrality

When you pay attention to your body and emotions in a deeper way, you will start to see things through the lens of neutrality. Nothing in the world is inherently good or bad. Everything is neutral. What happens is, as humans, we give meaning and assign emotions to our experiences. When we let these emotions override our systems, it disconnects us from alignment with our soul.

Before I left my corporate job, I found myself with an intense travel schedule that required a lot of time away, all while having two young girls at home. I grew frustrated with the additional travel and the amount of extra juggling it caused at home. In those moments, I blamed my job for these challenges. I also felt guilty and blamed myself for being away so much.

After many months, I chose to leave my job with mixed emotions, including frustration, anger, grief, and sadness. I also felt relief, freedom, and an openness to new possibilities I hadn't been able to fully process before. It took time for me to heal from that turning point in my life. With every step forward in building my own business, I was able to rediscover another part of myself. After all, there aren't many things as confronting on the personal growth journey as running your own business.

Looking back, I see that my challenging work situation was simply showing me I had outgrown that version of my life. I was entering a new phase that required more flexibility and freedom to make my schedule so that I could be home with my girls when needed (being present with my family is high on my values list).

By embracing neutrality, you're able to see the lessons that are meant for you. It can bring a new perspective and allow you to make clearer, more grounded decisions. This is an invitation to learn discernment and approach life lessons with a healthy detachment that allows you to keep going with the growth process.

Get curious and stay open to seeing what your contribution to a situation is. Every experience has something to learn from it. When you stay open to this, it will be easier to see things from a fresh perspective.

I've learned life is happening for me. Every experience is a gift. Understanding neutrality is a large part of how I arrived at this point. Now I'm able to navigate challenging situations with a deeper understanding of neutrality and the importance it brings to lessen stress and connect more deeply to my life.

Note: This isn't to diminish feelings and emotions that you have. It's important to get support and learn tools to help you navigate emotions, trauma, and other complex challenges you may be experience.

**Get curious in your life. You're invited to reflect on the
following questions:**

- Where do you assign emotions to things?
- What is your relationship with your emotions?
- Do you honor them and express them fully?
- Do you keep them bottled up?
- Do you dwell on things and then lash out?

_____

_____

_____

_____

_____

_____

_____

_____

_____

_____

Bring awareness to your current relationship with your emotions
as a way to work toward neutrality.

Ego

The ego is often associated with the negativity of someone that has a big ego. Meaning, they are full of or overly concerned with themselves. Because of this, we often think that the ego is bad and we try to ignore it or get rid of it. Ignoring it or wishing it away won't do you any good because it will still be there. You are not a bad person because you have an ego. The goal is to observe and work with the ego instead of letting it run the show.

The ego keeps most of us spinning in circles with negative self-talk by comparing ourselves to others, feeling that we aren't good enough, judging people or situations, and many other low expressions. It is the safe option in our mind that wants to feel in control.

Your ego is what gets in the way of neutrality. It is who you tell yourself you are without question. You true self is *I am*. Your ego is everything that comes after *I am*. I am smart. I am pretty. I am creative, etc.[1]

When you bring neutrality into your life, you are asking the ego to step aside. You can find ways to work with it by observing and looking for the lesson. Your ego is showing you where there is work to be done in order to fulfill your highest expression.

"Having a healthy ego means we can maintain a healthy sense of self, but an imbalance can lead to problems, including excessive self-centeredness."[2]

Observer Consciousness

Once you allow your emotions to come through and honor the fact that your feelings are valid, you can look deeper to understand observer consciousness. Observer consciousness is about putting your ego aside and recognizing that you are not your emotions. You are in a body with a beautiful mind and the possibility to feel a lot of feelings. When you practice being in the present moment, and you allow yourself to watch situations happening to you as an 'outsider', you have become an observer. You will see and understand a separateness from any given situation while also understanding that we (and everything) are all connected.

There is a story I was once told to explain observer consciousness. It goes like this:

A person is holding a string in their two hands.
The person then drops the string.
What's left?

Answer: The person watching the string. The observer.

When you are able to separate yourself from a situation as a way to see the growth or learning in it, you'll see your world differently. This is about is understanding your emotions, knowing your mind and ego are a part of the situation, and choosing to be an observer of your thoughts. This separation from your thoughts allows you to move deeper into a connection with your own soul. It allows you to feel your emotions, but not allow them to control you.

Most of the world is letting their emotions control and dictate their actions; however, stepping into observer consciousness, you'll see situations from a neutrality that brings more peace and understanding to your life.

Part 4: Key Takeaways

The Body

- The more intentional you are about building a healthy, loving relationship with your body, the more consistently you will be able to access your higher alignment.

- Pay attention to your energy. Learn to take care of and manage it. Don't allow others to take it from you.

- Listen to your Emotional Guidance System (EGS). It is always alerting you of where you're on track (feelings of joy, success, satisfaction, peace, etc.) versus where you have something to learn or get curious about (feelings of frustration, bitterness, anger, resentment, etc.).

- Release the stored emotions in your body regularly through somatic (body) exercises.

- Embrace a new way of being by becoming the Observer.

Additional Activities & Tools For The Body

Activity 4.3

Paying Attention To Your Body

Pay attention to your body. Journal on the following prompts to expand your relationship with your body.

Ask yourself:

- Do I give my body love on a regular basis?

- Do I have pain or stress that always shows up in a certain part of my body?

- What can I do to tune in and listen more to my body throughout my day?

_____

_____

_____

Activity 4.4

Self-Care For Your Body

There are many ways you can proactively take care of your body and give it more love. Below are a few body practices you can try:

- Stretching
- Movement / exercise
- Body Tapping
- Massages

Choose an activity you feel called to and start to experiment with it. If you're short on time, give yourself 5-10 minutes a day to explore and play with these modalities. You will begin to see that as you tune into your body, your relationship with it will heal and grow in new ways.

Tool 4.1

Body Tapping and Toe Tapping

Body Tapping is a powerful way to get out of your mind and into your body. It will wake up your meridian system and release stagnant energy. Brain & Body is a mind-body practice that originates in Korea. It combines stretching, flowing movement, and deep breathing exercises and meditation to connect more deeply with your body. I first learned about this concept in Ilchi Lee's book, *Water Up Fire Down.*[1]

Body Tapping:

Body tapping is really great for any time of day. Either as part of a morning or evening routine or as a break during the workday. You can pair it with relaxing music.

- Stand with your feet shoulder-width apart and in a relaxed position.
- Begin to gently tap the top of your head with your fingertips.

- As you take deep breaths, imagine breathing in fresh, clean air coming into your body as you inhale.
- Release any tension, stiffness, or negative, stagnant energy as you exhale.
- It is great to make noises as you release this energy. Whatever comes naturally to you during the process is great.
- Move to other parts of your body.
  - Tap the sides of your head.
  - Tap the back of your head.
  - Tap on your face: forehead, eyebrows, temples, around your eyes, nose, lips, cheeks, chin, and jaw.
  - Tap behind your ears.
  - Tap behind your head and neck.
  - Tap on your chest.
  - Tap your palms together.
  - Tap along your right arm from your shoulder down to your thumb and back up to your armpit.
  - Tap along your left arm in the same way.
  - Tap on your stomach (in the center and on both sides).
  - Tap on both sides of your lower back.
  - Tap down the back of your legs.
  - Tap your feet.
  - Tap up the front of your legs.
  - Tap on your hips.
  - Tap down the sides of your legs.
  - Tap your ankles.
  - Tap up the inside of your legs.
  - Tap your hips.
  - Tap your Don Jahn (two inches below your belly button).
  - Place your hands on your belly and take at least 3 deep breaths.

This 10 minute body tapping video provides more instructions.

This exercise is a really simple yet effective exercise to do from anywhere. As you feel into your body, you can go directly to the places you feel need the benefits of tapping. Trust what you feel and work with it.

Toe Tapping:

Toe tapping is another way to move the heat from your head (mental stress and chatter) and get more into your body.

- Lay down on the floor (a mat is recommended) with your legs shoulder-width apart.
- Set your arms to be about 45 degrees from your body.
- Tuck your chin slightly.
- Relax your back into the floor.
- Bring your heels together.
- Start to tap your toes together.
- Focus on tapping the inside of your big toes together.
- Find your own rhythm for tapping your toes together.
- Relax your body and your mind.
- As you take deep breaths, imagine breathing in fresh, clean air coming into your body as you inhale.
- Release any tension, stiffness, or negative, stagnant energy as you exhale.

- Bring your attention to your toes as you keep repeating the movement.
- When you complete your tapping, you can continue to lay there for an extra few minutes to let the tingling in your feet move into your body.

This 10 min toe tapping video provides more instructions.

This exercise may feel funny at first, but when you get used to it, it feels good. I have found it especially helpful for moving and releasing energy when I have headaches.

Additional Tapping Videos:

The BrainBodyTV channel has loads of other stuff. I recommend looking around and seeing what else you feel called to try.

Tool 4.2

Perform A Body Scan

Another way to connect with your body is by performing a body scan. This is a practice of noticing and breathing into different parts of your body. You can follow the below meditation to guide you as you breathe into different parts of your body and connect more deeply to yourself, or scan the QR code to download this meditation for free.

Note: It is best to do this activity in a quiet space, laying down if possible. Once you get used to working with this type of body scan, you'll be able to connect more quickly in the moment and can even practice it while you're on the go.

Body Scan Meditation:

- Lay down in a comfortable position with your arms and legs extended.
- Close your eyes.
- Take 3 deep, calm, cleansing breaths.
- Check in with every part of your body, starting with the top (crown) of your head.
- Breathe in and out as you notice how that part of your body is feeling. How does it feel? What does it need?
- Move on to the next part of your body.
- Check in with your forehead.
- Check in with your eyes. Behind your eyes.
- Check in with your ears, your nose, your mouth.
- Check in with your throat.
- Check in with your neck and chest.
- Check in with your shoulders.
- Check in with your right arm, your right elbow, your right wrist.
- Check in with your right hand and fingers.
- Check in with your left arm, your left elbow, your left wrist.
- Check in with your left hand and fingers.
- Check in with the palms of your hands.
- Check in with your heart.
- Check in with your ribcage.
- Check in with your organs—say hello to your kidneys, spleen, intestines.
- Check in with your lower abdomen.
- Check in with your pelvic area.
- Check in with your right thigh, your right knee, your right foot, and all of your toes.
- Check in with your left thigh, your left knee, your left foot, and all of your toes.
- Check in with the bottoms of your feet.

- Feel the energy pulsing from your body.
- Feel the energy pulsing around your body.
- Invite love and healing to any parts of your body that feel stiff, in pain, or have discomfort in any way.
- Imagine a white light entering the top of your head and flowing throughout your body.
- Allow this white light to fill all of your cracks and crevices, to merge with your bloodstream and to fill your body.
- Send love to all the parts of your body. Witness if you feel any tightness, heat, cold, or tingling and send light to that area.
- Imagine you are as light as a feather as you fill your body with this white light.
- Allow the white light to create peace and a sense of calm with your body and your system.
- Thank the white light for joining you on your healing journey. Whenever you feel discomfort, out of sorts or uneasy, call in this white light to guide you.
- Give thanks and gratitude to this white light and to your body for healing itself.
- Close with 3 deep, calm, cleansing breaths.

Reminder:

Your body is a temple. Treat it well.

Part 5:
The Soul

Understanding The Soul

Your soul lies deep within you and is your deepest essence and truest nature. It is the non-material piece of you that survives after the death of your physical body. Even though it is likely buried under layers of conditioning, limiting beliefs, and body numbing, it speaks to the purest form of you. The you that you came here to be. As you reprogram your mind and become more in tune with your body, you will begin to access your soul's wisdom. You may also refer to your soul as spirit, higher self, or high consciousness. I believe these are all connected, so please use what feels best to you.

Your soul came here with a specific mission. It came here to experience certain things and also contribute to society with your own specific gifts. As you live out your human experience, you'll come upon challenges that may bring you closer to your soul's mission, or lead you farther from it, depending on the choices you make. I am of the mindset that anytime you follow a feeling of excitement that truly lights you up (so long as it does not bring harm to others or have negative intentions), the more aligned you are with your soul's mission. When you make decisions that are driven by negative feelings and lower vibrations, you are moving away from your soul's calling. There is never any right or wrong—there is only what is. You always have a choice, and every moment is a new moment to choose.

Are you listening to the song of your soul? Do you allow the whispers to take up space and amplify within your being so you can truly recognize who you are, where you came from, and what you want out of this lifetime? Allow that power to show itself to you. Allow yourself to feel—deeply—into the joy your soul is asking for. Allow yourself to explore the wonders of your heart. It is from within the heart we carry our truest desires. These are not desires run by the ego or even the mind. They are not about what we *think* we want, or the wishes we have based on what others have. These are the deepest, truest inner speakings of our soul. The place that thrives when it is recognized as a power source of love for humanity. The place that amplifies gratitude and makes space for more connection, opportunity, and knowing deep within us. Listening to this voice is the greatest gift of a lifetime. To be truly connected to the voice of your soul and what it wants. After all, you came here to follow a path and learn what the soul wanted to learn. You already decided before you incarnated in this lifetime. You decided the tools in your toolkit (your gifts) and the lessons you wanted to learn. Life became a playing field to learn and expand. To go beyond the reaches of your lessons, to conquer them and evolve as a being.

What are you working on? What are you evolving through?

The soul knows. Your truest inner voice knows what it deeply desires. This comes from a place of love and devotion to the practice of living. To the gift of being a human on this planet in this lifetime. To experience the range of emotions—all the colors, options, and sizes of feelings you may have. After all, it is in these experiences we can feel in human form. The soul lives in a peaceful layer of existence that does not feel the density of the earth until it incarnates in human form.

Navigating Your Soul Expansion

Reflections in Your World

On your journey of life and growth, you will encounter many people. Some people will lead you toward your higher alignment, growth, and expansion, while others have the potential to lead you on a detour or the opposite direction. It is important to observe what is happening around you in order to determine how you respond.

Your outer world is a reflection of your inner world. Certain experiences and relationships happen to show or teach you something. As you begin to pay attention to that dynamic, you'll be able to navigate your experiences and relationships in different ways. We are all mirrors of each other. When someone causes a flood of emotions in you by something they say, do, or how they act, it is an invitation to look within yourself. It is an invitation to see what you are being asked to heal, and to sit with those feelings so you can work through them.

Pure intentions are a key part of staying in your alignment and accessing your soul's higher calling. Stay the course and hold clear intentions of who you are and what you want. Ensure it is in alignment with the highest good of all by being grounded in love. When you hold pure intentions, even if the relationships around you seem to crumble, you will stay connected to your true essence. Remember, you do not have to stay in situations that do not serve you. You can choose in any moment.

Relationships

As you strengthen your mind-body connection, you will change as a person. When that happens, there is a potential some of the people in your life will be uncomfortable with the person you are becoming. You may find you are no longer a vibrational match, as they will expect you to continue to be the version of you that you've outgrown and moved on from. If you are beginning to see the world with more beauty and wonder while others are complaining about everything around them, take it as a sign that you are expanding, even if it feels uncomfortable.

It can be helpful to seek out new connections and relationships that feel aligned to who you are now. This does not mean everything needs to be positive all the time. It means you are understanding a different way of being and operating that is more in alignment with how the universe works. You are here to learn, grow, and experience life. As you evolve, the people you surround yourself with will either grow with you or be left behind. Technically, they aren't left behind as much as still operating at a lower vibrational frequency.

Hold the highest intentions and trust your inner knowing. With that, you will be guided to people that are aligned with your path.

Spiritual Responsibility

As you strengthen your mind-body connection and become more conscious, you have a responsibility to use your gifts and your consciousness in ways that are most supportive to yourself and the work, not destructive or guided by the ego. I have met people on my path that are incredibly gifted yet also have more healing and growth to do in order to use their gifts responsibly. When I've been in those situations, I used my discernment to decide if I wanted to continue to have those people in my life or love them from afar.

We all have healing to do, myself included, and it lasts our whole lives, so this is not out of judgment. I say it as a way to remind you to use discernment in your life and in your relationships. Not everyone is going to serve your highest good. It's not that it's good or bad, but it's important to be aware of this, so you continue to make decisions for yourself. No one else can make your decisions for you. You might let them, but in the end, if it's not in alignment for you, it will probably not end well.

Do not let anyone else dictate your life. You may make compromises sometimes out of love for others, however, this should not be at the expense of yourself. It can be very easy to get caught up in situations where people are using others for their benefit. Not everyone that works with consciousness is in their highest alignment. It is important to remember this and never rely on someone else for your own work. Even while reading this book, who am I to say what is best for you? I'm not. I'm here to share tools, expand your awareness, and open you up to other possibilities. I'm not here to tell you what to do. Please use discernment and find what feels correct for you on your path.

Blocks To Your Soul

Not everything related to your spiritual evolvement is sunshine and roses. It is important to be mindful of people and situations that do not fit for you. The easiest way to understand this is by observing how you feel in any given situation. If a person ignores your life experiences and tries to get you to feel overly optimistic in every situation or twist your words in the name of development, be alert to their motives. If a person constantly makes you feel you must follow their lead, it is a signal you may be too closely tied to them. These are scenarios and situations that block your own alignment to your soul's calling.

Spiritual Bypassing

Spiritual bypassing is the process of ignoring someone's experiences or feelings while redirecting them to be positive at all times. For example, if you suffered from abuse as a child and a person's solution for that is to tell you to ignore that experience because it is in the past, it would be wise to reconsider your relationship with them.

Note: When you have deep wounds and complex trauma you are trying to heal from, you may find it beneficial to first seek out the help of a licensed professional.

Leaders and Followers

Be mindful of anyone who enters your life and expects you to follow their lead. In the spiritual space, this is someone that considers themselves a Guru. The thing is, you are not here to be a follower of someone else. You are here to be your own leader of your life.

You may really love the way someone teaches a specific topic or feel they can help you in many ways. It is absolutely ok to consider someone a teacher that you learn from and trust for guidance. It becomes a slippery slope when you become dependent on that relationship and, over time, find yourself reliant on them in order to make decisions for yourself.

As someone that has always been a seeker, I have searched for people that could tell me more about who I am. Perhaps they were clairvoyant or a seer that could tell me things about what I was navigating in my life. It is fun to see things and connect with the spirit world, of course. It becomes tricky when you rely on that information and don't filter it through your own discernment. Be very hesitant about getting too close with anyone that makes promises for how your life will turn out or if they make demands for how connected you stay to them.

You are on this journey to experience and navigate life with your own self sovereignty. You have a gift of always being in control of your decisions. Do not let anyone try to convince you otherwise.

Recognizing Recurring Patterns In Your Life

As you reflect on where you're at in your life, you may notice certain themes, cycles, or patterns keep repeating themselves. These patterns are usually an indication of something you're here to work through, learn, and break free from. Oftentimes, it's something unpleasant that you didn't even want to happen.

Whether it's a certain type of relationship, or a similar theme recurring with your work, these are cycles and patterns that usually indicate we haven't learned a lesson in that area yet. There is likely a different angle or perspective to take from what is happening. Perhaps it is to stand in your power more and speak your voice. It could also be to detach from a specific type of person and practice self-sovereignty. Whatever the reason is, let the repeat scenarios be a guide for you to reflect in deeper ways.

You likely can't fully move on to the next phase of your life until you learn the lesson, break that pattern, and choose something different.

Identifying these patterns, breaking them, and choosing

something new is what you're here to do. That is how you're going to get through your next transformation and achieve a significant life change.

The first step is recognizing the patterns.

Here is an example of a pattern you may relate to. One of my clients had a pattern of telling herself she was not worth it in some way. When she came to work with me, she was questioning herself and where she was with her work. She'd ask questions like, "I love what I do, but I have trouble talking about it with others. I don't feel like I know enough to be an expert." The reality was, she had decades of experience. The only difference was now she was working on her own business instead of within a company. We had to work through her old beliefs, reprogram them from her mind, reconnect her with her body, and get her used to operating from a soul level in order to grow her business and reach her financial goals.

You may already be familiar with certain patterns you tell yourself. Some of the more common ones include imposter syndrome and comparing yourself to others.

I invite you to reflect on the following questions:

- What are the patterns in your life?
- What are the cycles in your life that keep you stuck at a certain level?

_____

_____

_____

_____

_____

You might feel you've made progress when you break through a certain block, only to see the same pattern come up again in a slightly different way. Don't worry. This is all part of the process. Continue to show up and use the tools in your toolkit to uncover your next step.

Patterns can also show up in relationships. Many of us are tied to relationships with people that hold us back in some way. Maybe you have someone in your life that doesn't believe in you or someone that is making you believe you can't live without them. Relationships are complex and at the end of the day, you are here in this life as yourself to live out your highest expression. Don't let anyone hold you back from that.

Years ago, I had a friend and mentor in the spiritual space. I learned many beautiful things from this person who expanded my concept of the universe and working more deeply with my soul's calling. Unfortunately, I came to realize that my friend had some challenging behaviors. I noticed manipulation happening and eventually downright lies that impacted people I care deeply about. When that happened, I chose to step away because their actions didn't align with my values. After some reflection and apologies on their part, we tried to continue our work together and our friendship. Unfortunately, a few additional instances happened and then I had to say goodbye for good.

I share this story because it can be painful to let go. Especially when you love deeply and want the best for people. The thing is, if people don't want to change, you can't make them change. And if they don't change time and time again, eventually you may need to cut ties for your own well-being.

My situation was not nearly the level of manipulation that I know many people go through—especially people in abusive relationships or in cults of any sort.

Looking back, my friend was probably overwhelmed with life and hadn't figured out a way to comfortably cope with it. What I had to realize was that it's ok. Their actions and behaviors are their choice. My actions and behaviors are my own.

Forgiveness is a powerful process. If you are holding onto a relationship or harboring feelings that aren't serving you, it may be time to take a deeper look and heal on your terms so you can move forward in your life.

This experience completely changed the trajectory of my life in many ways. The wisdom I learned is a big part of how and why I'm the person I am and why I'm able to write this book today. Even when lessons are painful, there can also be beauty in the process.

Activity 5.1

Identifying Patterns

1. Make a list of patterns that keep you stuck—it can be phrases you tell yourself or experiences you've seen play out in relationships, work, etc.
2. Pick one of those patterns to reflect on and see where it has led you over the years in your life.
3. Brainstorm how you can change your approach with this pattern to break it for good.

Some recurring patterns you might struggle with could be:

- I don't know enough about _____. How could anyone want me to speak/write/teach about it?
- I can't move forward because I don't know enough.
- I am not worthy of _____.
- I have to prove myself.
- What if I make a mistake?
- What will other people think?
- I'm not as good as this other person, so what's the point of even trying?
- I'm too embarrassed or scared to put myself out there.

You have the ability to choose something different for yourself. You can decide that XYZ is not your story anymore. You can let that story go and choose something different. Write a different story about who you are and what you want.

_____

_____

_____

_____

_____

_____

_____

_____

_____

_____

_____

_____

_____

The Continued
Depths Of Gratitude

As you deepen your appreciation for your life and practice gratitude on a regular basis, you will see the world around you change. This will also deepen your awareness and level of capacity to see the beauty around you. When you connect with your soul, the depth of your gratitude will leave you awestruck.

Have you ever felt gratitude for Earth?

One day, I went for one of my daily walks and it was a sunny, beautiful day. I stopped at one spot on my walk where you can see a view of the mountains. The sky was really clear and everything looked so beautiful. I was struck with how amazing Earth is. It was overwhelming in the moment—the thought of, Wow, how incredible is it that we're here? How incredible is it that we're on this vibrant, beautiful, colorful, magnificent planet? How amazing is it that we get to see these blue skies, shining sun, green grass, chirping birds, snow, and rain?

I pictured looking at the Earth from space alongside other

planets. I've seen photos many times, but in that moment, it really hit me. The universe looks dark from space and Earth looks so vibrant because of all of the water and nature and living beings on the planet. The other planets don't really have that since they are not inhabitable.

We get to experience all these different temperatures and climates and we get to experience the seasons (if you live somewhere where you can see the seasons more clearly). We see the death and rebirth of nature—watching life grow, die, and sprout again. It's really magnificent.

This experience stayed with me because I felt it deep in my body. I saw the vastness of it, and I felt how big of a thing this is, where we're living, and what this world looks like.

There are a lot of things that are sad about the state of the world. There is a lot that Earth is showing us in relation to climate change and global warming. Reminders that we need to take care of her more.

Are you paying attention to and cultivating an appreciation for what you have in this moment? Or are you getting sucked into your daily life, going through your routines and your schedules, rushing out the door, going to work, rushing back in the door, rushing through dinner, and going to bed?

Don't get me wrong, I have times where I want to just get through the day. Especially with young kids at home, it can feel like a lot is happening at once. It's another part of the human experience.

Yes, you will have moments that feel extremely busy and also, how can you have the moments of feeling grateful, appreciative, and recognizing the wonder and the beauty in the world?

Allow yourself to reflect on that. Explore your relationship with gratitude. See where you feel wonder and awe within your life. Having this mindset will shift everything for you.

You're invited to sit with and explore your relationship with gratitude:

- What does gratitude look like?
- What does gratitude feel like?
- How do you practice gratitude?
- How can you invite more gratitude into your life?

_____

_____

_____

_____

_____

_____

_____

_____

_____

_____

_____

_____

_____

_____

_____

_____

_____

_____

_____

_____

_____

_____

_____

There is a video on social media of an adult seeing snow for the first time in his life. He was so excited. He was filled with love, joy, and amazement for the snow. He ran his fingers through it with wonder and awe. If you're used to seeing snow, you could very easily complain about snow and talk about the dangers of driving in it or of black ice. This video was such a great reminder that it's all about perspective. Do not take the little things for granted.

What allows you to connect deeper in ways that feel incredible to you?

The Power Of Prayer

A great way to connect with your highest self is to invite prayer into your life. Prayer has different meanings to different people and I do recognize there can be heavy emotions that come with it—especially if you have experience with a specific religion tied to your childhood, for example. In this case, when I speak about prayer, I mean for it to be on your terms and aligned with what you believe in.

Prayer is not only about asking for things that you want. Prayer also includes gratitude for what you have. In fact, it is recommended that more than half of your time spent in prayer focuses on what you are grateful for in your life. That way, you can stay grounded in seeing the beauty of where you are now while also setting intentions for your future.

Prayer does not have to be religious in nature. If you feel weight to it due to past experiences, I invite you to try to set that aside and look at prayer as a neutral path that allows you to connect with your higher self.

Prayer is a way for you to connect with your spirit guides and guardians, and set intentions for where you'd like to go in the future. It can be as simple as recognizing what you are grateful for (covered earlier in Part 5) and naming your deepest desires for your life going forward. Keep in mind, this is best to not be strictly material things. It is meant to relate to the feelings you have and who you want to be in the world.

Activity 5.2

Sample Prayer

Allowing yourself to connect with prayer can start to create a new relationship between you, your soul, and your guides. This is a process I continuously work on. The more I open myself up to prayer and have a daily relationship with my guides, the easier I find it to notice synchronicities and identify when I am getting messages from the other realms.

Being sincere in your message goes a long way toward truly connecting to your guides. Be honest with where you are and what you're grateful for.

Sample prayer outline:

- Start by clapping your hands 3 x 3, 3 rounds of 3 claps each round (9 claps total) to open the prayer.
- Welcome in your spirit guides and guardians.
- Communicate what you are grateful for in the present moment within your life.
- Communicate any intentions you have for the direction of your life or your deepest desires.

- Thank your guides for being with you.
- Clap your hands 3 x 3, 3 rounds of 3 claps each round (9 claps total) to close the prayer.

Below is a sample of some things you may say in a prayer. However, remember to make it your own in any ways you feel called to do so.

Dearest Guides, Guardians, Ancestors, and Angels,

I welcome you into this space to support and guide me for the highest good of all.

I am deeply grateful for what I have in my life, the lessons I have learned, and the experiences I am navigating. Even when things feel hard, I know there is a deeper purpose to what I am moving through.

My intention with this prayer is to communicate my gratitude and love for all. I love you and appreciate your protection in my life. I know that I am on my path. That this is part of my soul's journey. Even when the road feels hard, I am protected and loved unconditionally.

Please continue to watch out for me as I navigate my path, support me and guide me as I live this lifetime.

Thank you.

Seeing Synchronicity

Have you ever thought of someone and the next moment they called you?

That is because we are all connected on energetic and vibrational levels. As you expand your awareness, you will see synchronicities in your life. These are little nudges from the universe to show you that you are on your path. They can be things like seeing certain repeating numbers, symbols, or even animals that cross your path.

When you may be questioning yourself, seeing these synchronicities can be a way to stay encouraged and trust your journey. Since the spirit world cannot sit down and have a chat with you in the standard human way, your guides will use signs and symbols to remind you they are with you and you are always divinely guided.

As I become more open to this work, I am able to see synchronicities all the time (throughout my day) and it doesn't surprise me anymore. It is a way of knowing I am following my highest aligned path.

My dear friend Cindy once told me that *"separation is an illu-*

sion" and it stayed with me. We are all intertwined. The work you do ripples out into the world. By you finding your way and making your mark, you will leave a lasting impact. I believe this is the work of the soul. Being a human in this lifetime is the most immense and intense kind of growth a soul can experience and a gift to the world.

Part 5: Key Takeaways

The Soul

- Connecting to your soul is a process of getting out of your mind, into your body, and tuning into your higher frequency.

- You are a miracle. Own this belief as you walk this world.

- Pay attention to any repeating patterns in your life. They are keys to showing you where your lessons and growth are held.

- Prayer and gratitude are powerful ways to connect with a feeling greater than yourself.

- Find ways to connect with your soul and you will create your life from a completely different place.

Additional
Activities & Tools
For The Soul

Activity 5.3

What is your soul yearning for?

Along this journey, you may encounter a lot of noise, doubt, or uncomfortable curiosity from loved ones or others that are close to you. That is to be expected. What matters is how much you allow this noise to impact you.

When you stay strong in your mind-body connection, your soul will pull you forward one step at a time. Keep this in mind as you face any challenges.

It's time to explore your soul's calling.

What is your deepest desire, dream, or wish you have for yourself in this lifetime?

Who do you want to be?

What do you want to accomplish?

Take some time to reflect on these questions. Journal, go for a walk, or even talk to yourself out loud if you're an external processor. Find what works best for you to get into your creativity and dream state and use that as a starting point.

Even if it seems unattainable, it is a dream in your heart for a reason. Follow that and honor it. Remember, don't judge yourself about how big or unrealistic your dream might be, or worry about what others may think.

This is YOUR process and YOUR journey. Nothing is off limits.

_____

_____

_____

_____

_____

_____

_____

_____

_____

_____

_____

_____

Activity 5.4

Re-Write Your Soul Story

What do you want your story to look like?

Anything that happened to you in the past, you're making it mean something about yourself. When you hold on to what you think it means about you, that keeps you stuck and stops you from doing what you really want to do.

What is a story you tell yourself that is holding you back in your life?

Write it down.

Now, review it and rewrite it the way you wish it was happening.

For example, if you have a story of never feeling valued, write what your life would be like if you felt valued in every moment. How would you feel, be, and act?

As you uncover your patterns and work with them in

different ways, you will shift your energy and be able to create in a different way.

Consider this an invitation to reflect on the places where you may feel stuck, lost, or in a pattern that is on repeat over and over and over again. Then, take a look at how you can change that pattern. How can you shift those thoughts?

When you make the conscious choice and put effort into changing something in your life, you will start to feel freedom. The larger of an impact you will make. You will move through the world differently. The possibilities are endless.

_____

_____

_____

_____

_____

_____

_____

_____

_____

_____

_____

_____

_____

_____

_____

_____

_____

_____

_____

_____

_____

_____

_____

_____

_____

_____

_____

Tool 5.1

Working With The Four Elements

The four elements of Earth, Air, Fire, and Water are what make up all of creation. Bringing your awareness to the elements and connecting with them is a great way to access your soul. I personally love to walk in nature (Earth) and feel the wind (Air) as I walk. There is a river (Water) near my house that is always flowing. It is a great reminder to stay in the energy of flow for creation. Depending on the time of year, there may be smoke (Fire) from chimneys in the winter, or the bright sun (also Fire) in the summer. Recognizing and connecting with the four elements always reminds me we are all connected. Along with that, we are such a small (yet powerful and impactful) part of the universe. Whenever fear, doubt, or anxiety creep into your mind, connecting to something 'bigger' than yourself will help to move through those lower vibrational feelings.

You can also invite in the four elements to your workspace to connect more deeply to your creativity. Setting up an area in your space with items representing each of the elements can help keep them on your radar and in your mind as you are working.

Below are some ways to connect with each of the elements in your home or workspace:

- Earth – crystals for energy and healing, flowers, plants

- Air – open your windows to get fresh air and feel the wind

- Water – place a small bowl of water at your work station

- Fire – light candles or incense to ignite a spark and create a lovely smelling atmosphere

Visualization can have a powerful and profound effect on our state of being. Take a moment to visualize one of the following scenes as a way to ground yourself with all four of the elements.

If you are someone that enjoys the **beach,** follow this scene:

- Take 3 deep, calm, cleansing breaths.
- Imagine you are standing on the beach, looking out to the sea.
- Feel the sand move between your toes.
- Feel the strength and stability of the earth beneath your feet.
- Feel the flow of the water as it rushes to the shore and greets you.
- Feel the wind gently whirling around your face.
- Feel the power of the sun beating down on you, igniting your being.

Sit with this feeling of being on the beach and connecting to the four elements. Notice what else you see and feel around you.

Invite the elements to speak to you. Allow them to show you the grandness of this planet and how we are all connected.

If you prefer to be in the **mountains**, follow this scene:

- Take 3 deep, calm, cleansing breaths.
- Imagine you are sitting at a campfire in the mountains.
- Observe the trees standing tall around you.
- Feel the earth, grass, and leaves underneath you.
- Hear the steady flow of the nearby stream.
- Hear the gentle rustling of the leaves as the wind greets you.
- Feel the warmth of the campfire.
- Feel the stillness in the air from a secluded spot.

Sit with this feeling of being in the mountains and connecting to the four elements. Notice what else you see and feel around you. Invite the elements to speak to you. Allow them to show you the grandness of this planet and how we are all connected.

Scan the QR code to download The Beach and The Mountain meditations for free.

Tool 5.2

Breathing Through Your Entire Body

Another way to connect within is by noticing and breathing into different parts of your body. You can follow the below meditation to guide you as you breathe into different parts of your body and connect deeper to yourself, or scan this QR code to download the meditation for free.

Note: It is best to do this activity in a quiet space, laying down if possible. Once you get used to working with this type of body check in, you'll be able to connect more quickly in the moment and can even practice it while you're on the go.

Body Breathing Meditation:

- Lay down in a comfortable position with your arms and legs extended.
- Close your eyes.
- Take 3 deep, calm, cleansing breaths.
- Breathe in and out of each part of your body.
- Feel the movement as you bring awareness to that area.

How does it feel?
What does it need?

- Breathe into the top of your head.
- Breathe into your face.
- Breathe into your neck.
- Breathe into your shoulders.
- Breathe into your chest.
- Breathe into your arms.
- Breathe into your wrists.
- Breathe into the palms of your hands.
- Breathe into your ribcage.
- Breathe into your stomach.
- Breathe into your intestines.
- Breathe into your kidneys.
- Breathe into your belly button.
- Breathe into your hips.
- Breathe into your thighs.
- Breathe into your knees.
- Breathe into your shins.
- Breathe into your calves.
- Breathe into your ankles.
- Breathe into your heels.
- Breathe into your toes.
- Breathe into the bottoms of your feet.

Feel the breath entering and leaving your body from each place. As you breathe through the various parts of your body, you will feel a connection to your body and your presence on a deeper level. Allow this presence to awaken your soul.

Observe what comes up, and how you feel as you connect in this space.

Give thanks and gratitude to your soul for its guidance on your journey.

Close with 3 deep, calm, cleansing breaths.

Reminder:

What is meant for you will make its way to
you . . . if you allow it.

Part 6:
Integration

Living Your Mind-Body Soul Aligned Life

Integration is the process of incorporating new pieces of information into your life. It is a critical part of any transformation. Not only is it the process of learning something as a form of knowledge, but it's about how you take that information and do something with it to change your life. It is embodying a new version of yourself.

Integration comes in many forms and is a lifelong process. You may have a season of integration where it feels like life is moving fast and you're changing a lot. You may have other seasons where things seem to move slowly and you aren't sure if any change is being made. Change is always happening, whether it seems obvious to you in the moment, or not. Keep your end goal in mind. Stay focused on being in your highest expression.

Making Daily
Aligned Choices

I t can feel challenging to make decisions and yet, it's an important part of living in your highest alignment. You have your own unique way of choosing what is most aligned for you. Most people make decisions using their mind, however, decisions are meant to be made with the body.

Have you ever had a situation where you got a gut instinct about something, but ignored that feeling and in the end, your instinct had been right? That's because your body knows the answer before your mind does. What usually happens is the body gets ignored and the mind takes over. Now that you've learned about the mind-body connection, you can begin using it in your life. A great place to start is by how you make decisions.

Human Design is a tool I use with clients to learn more about their individual decision-making style. It highlights how their body wants to operate naturally without the mind's interference. Over the years, I have experimented with my own decision-making process and it absolutely changed my life. I am able to recognize so much more about myself and what truly feels like the best decision for me, without my ego getting in the way. I have seen firsthand this impact for my clients, and it is transformational. When you put this information into practice, it moves you to operate in a way that is more in alignment with who you truly are.

To learn more about how Human Design may benefit your life, scan the QR code below.

Building Emotional Resilience & Consistency

Creating Boundaries

One of the hardest things I found when starting this work was being able to say no. I always wanted to be everywhere, doing everything. Sometimes I felt bad to say no to an event, even if I really didn't want to go. I didn't want to hurt anyone's feelings. It did get a little easier to say no when I became a parent. Probably because my time was more limited. However, it was still a practice to learn about boundaries and then really set my own. Setting boundaries as a mom also meant finding time for me. Not for work, and not to be parenting, but for myself to do as I pleased. Whether it was taking time to journal, walk, or try out a new hobby, I needed time for myself. In order to find that time, I had to start saying no to other things.

I believe this is critical for every single person in the world. Taking time for yourself to explore and experiment with things you enjoy—without the need to justify it or share it with others—is crucial. We'd all be a little less stressed and definitely happier if this time was built into our days. Unfortunately, it's usually an afterthought, and most regularly, the first thing to get removed from the list when there is too much going on in our lives. I get it, I really do. You can't predict when a child will get sick or when something big will come up at work. The thing is, you still need time for yourself. Think about this—if you try to take care of everyone else, but you haven't taken care of yourself —how will you be showing up? Likely from an exhausted, stressed out place. The more you can incorporate taking time for yourself, the better off you'll be.

Forming Habits

Making lasting change can feel hard and part of what makes it harder is the need to change your habits. In order to show up in the world differently, we need to choose to take different actions. Part of this is creating habits to support you in who you are becoming.

For example, if you want to write a book, it is very unlikely you will go from not writing at all to one day having a fully written manuscript. Your first step might be to take a writing class or start writing for 10 minutes a day. Showing up consistently and creating new habits is how you make the *leap* from not writing at all to having a full manuscript.

There is a saying that in order to create the life you want, it will cost you your old one. You have to choose a different path in order to disrupt what you've always done and get new results.

Some tips for creating new habits include:

Integrate one new habit at a time.

I see a lot of people trying to change their whole life in one day (i.e. setting a New Year's resolution). They end up breaking the habit within a few days or a week because it is too much to keep up with. Start with one new habit and make it part of your routine. If you want to start writing for 10 minutes a day (keeping with the writing example), then set a time in your calendar and stick to it. If you're a morning person, perhaps you want to wake up 10 minutes earlier and write as soon as you wake up. If you have a hard time getting up in the morning and it doesn't feel enticing enough to wake up earlier, perhaps you set a timer for noon every day and pause for 10 minutes to write. Reflect on how you work and find what works best for you.

Know your why.

Know why you have the goal. If you want to write a book because it is your lifelong dream to become a published author, remember that every time you find it hard to sit and write. You are more likely to stick with your new habit if you are deeply connected to why you're doing it. Otherwise, it is easy to question the point of it all and give up in a moment when you're not feeling great.

Create a ritual around your new habit.

At the time you go to write, create a ritual that will make it fun for you to sit at your desk. Maybe it's making a cup of your favorite tea or putting on music that helps you focus. I personally love to pull up a playlist of instrumental music any time I sit down to write. My brain is now trained to be ready to write in that environment.

Starting Small

An important part of starting any new habits is to start small. Don't try to add 5 or 10 new habits at the same time. Pick ONE item that you want to work on.

It can take anywhere from 18 to 254 days to form a new habit with an average of 66 days.[1] Please don't get discouraged.

Unlocking your mind-body connection is an ever-evolving process. The important thing is to pick something and start. Remember that in every moment, you have a choice. So even if you get off track, you can pick back up in your next moment.

Disconnecting from Devices

Our devices hold access to the world and an infinite amount of information at our fingertips. The average person checks their phone at least 58 times per day and spends 4 hours and 37 minutes on their device.[2] What you consume stays within your brain and body as memories. It gives your mind fuel for whatever patterns it wants to hold on to as true (usually negative ones). As you take in and absorb all of that information, it can overrun your thoughts. It is important to disconnect from your phone regularly and create space for yourself.

If you find it difficult to detach from your phone (or other devices), experiment with some of the following options:

- Set time limits for apps
- Charge your phone in a different room
- Turn off notifications
- Remove addictive apps from your phone
- Use your phone in grayscale (instead of color)—it will make you want to be on it less

It's important to be aware of your relationship with your phone (and other electronic devices). Do you want to change how often you interact in this way? If so, pay attention to how you currently use these devices and identify what you wish your relationship would be instead. Once you do that, you can see what types of small changes you need to make in order to get there.

Celebrating Small Wins

I'm a firm believer in celebrating your small wins. I'd probably go so far as to say it's even more important than celebrating the big wins. Yes, big wins are amazing. However, they don't happen as often as the small wins. Celebrating the small wins is what will help keep you going when you're not feeling great and need an extra little push. These wins allow you to create a closer connection with your everyday life and really embrace your path. Other people may celebrate you along the way, but the person that is most important in your process is you. It's important that you celebrate you.

A great way to keep track of your wins (big and small) is by making a list. You can use a notes app on your phone, a Google doc, or even a pen and paper. No need to make it a cumbersome task. Use a system you already have in place for other things in your life. Create a list and then each time something great happens, note it down on the list. You'll be surprised at how quickly things add up when you're looking out for them. The added benefit is that keeping a list will help you remember these great things down the road. If you're having a moment where you aren't feeling great or having a bad day, take a look at your list. Celebrate all of your wins and recognize how far you've come.

Planning Your Day:
Find What Works For You

Morning Rituals

M orning rituals are an important way to connect to your inner self before entering the busy-ness of the day. Your mind is clearest when you first wake up after a night of restful sleep. Most of us wake up and the first thing we do is grab our phone—usually to read emails or check social media before getting out of bed. When this happens, we are already putting inputs into our mind before we've had a chance to connect to ourselves.

There are a lot of great, simple options to connect with yourself first thing in the morning.

- Take 3 deep breaths
- Say 3 things you're grateful for out loud
- Check in with your body by doing a body scan
- Ask yourself, *What do I need today?*

- Do a few yoga poses (supports breathing and stretching to awaken the body)

I encourage you to test out different morning routines to see what works best for you. If you struggle to find time in the morning, consider choosing one activity you'd like to try. Commit to doing that one activity first thing when you wake up for at least 21 days. You can always build upon that one activity at a later time.

Evening Routines

Evening routines are a helpful way to wind down and let your body know it's time to rest. I enjoy calming activities at this time of day in order to mentally and physically prepare for bed. This can include light stretching, meditation, journaling, reading (preferably not on a screen), or even listening to calming music.

The evening is also a great time to reflect on how your day went. You can ask yourself questions such as:

- What went well today?
- What could have gone better?
- What am I grateful for that happened today?

Taking time to reflect on the self and your day invites you to get into the habit of self-reflection.

Activity: Crafting Your Morning Ritual & Evening Routine

If you want to be more intentional with your time, a great place to start is with your morning and evening routines.

Start by observing your current morning and evening routines. You may not think you have any (at least not intentionally), but if you observe yourself over a few days, you will start to see patterns, I promise. Maybe you pick up your phone first thing to check your email after your alarm goes off. Or maybe you go directly to the bathroom to brush your teeth. You likely have an order that you already stick to for getting ready in the morning. Take time to observe it all and write it down if that's helpful.

Then, choose one thing you'd like to change and identify what you want to replace it with. Do you want to stop checking your email first thing in the morning? (Highly recommended, for sure.) You can buy an old fashion alarm clock or use an old phone that isn't connected to the internet to set your morning wake-up time. That allows you to keep your working phone in another room while you sleep and you can get up and get ready without checking your phone. If that seems like a stretch, start with something else. Maybe instead, take 3 conscious breaths as soon as you wake up and say to yourself, *It's going to be a great day today.*

The idea is to observe what you're doing now, identify what you want to do differently, and then determine how you're going to make that change. Once it feels like you have a handle on that change, see if there is anything else you'd like to change in your morning or evening routines. As always, find what works for you.

Activity: Brain Breaks

As much as we are programmed to think humans can operate 24/7, that is simply not the case. The average adult's attention span is 8.25 seconds.[1] With the increase of phone use, along with social media, our attention spans continue to decline over time.

The Pomodoro® Technique is one way to set up your time to include brain breaks. This framework suggests you work for 25 minutes, and then take a 5-minute break. After four 25-minute work sessions, give yourself a longer, 20- or 30-minute break.[2]

Add brain breaks into your day. Set a timer throughout the

day where you can take a 1 minute pause and check in with yourself.

Some activities you can do include:

- Get up from your desk and stretch your body
- Close your eyes and take deep breaths
- Close your eyes and focus on the dark space in the middle of your forehead, between your eyes (third eye)
- Go outside to stand in the grass
- Go for a walk
- Get a drink of water

Overcoming Obstacles

I recognize mind-body work may come more easily to some people than others. I also recognize it can take time and dedication to really shift things in your life. After all, if you've been operating a certain way for 10, 20, or even 30+ years, it's likely you won't see big change happen overnight.

That's ok. This book is about making changes however you can. Small, incremental changes are usually more impactful than one big change. Over time, you can experiment and see what works for you and what doesn't. You can build new habits that become part of who you are instead of trying to follow a quick fix formula. How many New Year's resolutions have you broken before the end of January? Don't worry, we all have. This section will focus on ways your brain might try to self-sabotage you (i.e. stop you from making the progress you truly desire) along with ideas for overcoming those challenges.

When You're Short On Time

Time is important for everyone and it's usually something

we're always trying to find more of—to no avail. I will ask you to have an open mind and find 1, 2, or 5 minutes to spare for a quick exercise.

- You can name 3 things you're grateful for while walking into work.
- You can take the stairs for a little extra movement in your day.
- You can repeat affirmations to yourself out loud in the car.

All these things may seem so small and insignificant because they don't take up a lot of time. However, their impact is not proportionate to how long you spend doing them. Of course, if you spend more time on them, you may see results faster or in a different way. But even 1 minute a day can have an impact. And if you're really looking for your minutes, you can take 1 minute in the morning and another in the afternoon. It's really about catching yourself in moments where you can make a connection, even if it's short.

When You Feel Stuck

There is a fine line between feeling stuck and procrastination. On the one hand, sometimes when you're stuck, you need a break. It means you aren't in flow and you could use some time away to gain perspective. At some point, though, that stagnation can be an excuse for procrastination. Are you really not on the right path and not in alignment, or are you afraid of what will come next if you do succeed? We can't be in flow 100% of the time, but there are things that can support you to be more in flow. Perhaps setting up a pre-work ritual with things like sitting in a specific place within your house, lighting candles, playing focused music, or making a cup of tea before you begin. All these things can support shifting your mood from stuck to focused and taking action.

A mentor once told me action brings clarity. That stayed with me because even when we feel stuck, there is always a way to move out of it. When we stay in a mode of overthinking or over-worrying about something, it is keeping us where we are. When you really aren't sure of how things will work out, you still need to take a step. If you don't, you'll stay in your overthinking or overworrying mode.

You really only ever need one moment to make a choice to shift things.

When you feel stuck, reflect on the following:

- What can you put into place to support yourself when you feel stuck?

- How can you get yourself to take a form of action, even one small step, to keep you moving?

When I know I need a break, I will take a walk, stretch, or move on to another activity for a while. I've gained enough self-awareness at this point that I know when I'm putting something off because I don't want to do it, while also knowing it is the thing that needs to get done in order to advance my goal.

Ask yourself:

- Will your future self thank you for what you're doing right now?

This question has propelled me forward many times. Even in times of writing this book (a labor of love) because I knew this book was an important part of my future.

There is so much power in self-awareness. A lot of people shy away from it because they are afraid of what they might say. But not you, dear reader, for you are reading this book. Embrace all the parts of yourself and be kind to yourself as you move through this process.

When You Break Your Habit

Let's say you've been implementing some of these strategies for a few weeks, and then something happens and you get sidetracked. Maybe there's an illness or injury at home, or a short trip throws you off your routine. The important thing to remember is that it's never too late to start again. Just because you miss a day, or two or three, doesn't mean you are doomed forever. Our brains like to put us in 'all or nothing' scenarios, but that's not the reality of life. The reality is, things happen. Stuff comes up, and it takes us off course sometimes. The important thing is what you choose in the next moment. Do you choose to say: *I got thrown off and I can't get back to it* or *I've done it before and I can do it again, starting now?* Your desire to change has to be stronger than your desire to stay the same. This is how you can break free from old programming, start again, and keep creating something new for yourself.

Inconsistency

To go along with the 'all or nothing' thought in breaking habits, inconsistency is something that comes up for a lot of people. You may be one of them. One day you might be all in and do 5 self-care activities from your list, and the next day, you do nothing. It's ok if this happens. The key is to recognize where you are and take it from there. Choose one thing to be consistent with every day. Even if that activity is only for 1 minute a day. Then, treat anything else you're able to do that day as icing on the cake. That way, if there is a day where you feel like you can't do much, you can focus on doing just the one thing for 1 minute.

As you start to develop and grow these practices, you'll see yourself shifting your priorities to make more space for this type of work.

Past Disappointments

There are always times in our life when we wish we would have done things differently. Past disappointments and regrets often get in the way of where we want to go in the future. We hold on to the memories and pain of something in the past and it stops us from moving forward. If you find yourself stuck in this way, you will need to move through that pain in order to heal and grow. You'll need to realize your past doesn't dictate your future, and it's time to make new decisions.

What's done is done. Now is your chance to do something differently. You are reading this book as a way to choose yourself, so consider this your next step in the process. Identify what might be holding you back from the past. Accept and recognize that it happened. Forgive yourself for what happened. Forgive others if others are involved. Recognize that you are in a different place now and it is time to let go in order to grow.

It's easy to hold on to shame and blame of the past. When you release this and truly let go of it, you can step into your creative way of being. We are not on Earth to feel stuck and weighed down by regret and worry. When you recognize this, you can move on. Creation comes from getting out of the mind and into the body. Anytime you feel stuck, go back to the body exercises in Part 4: The Body and pick one to try. The more often you choose a new path, the more ease you will have in sticking with it.

You may also have a hard time believing that possibilities are available to you. It's important to realize the world is full of possibilities to the degree you so choose. If you don't believe something is possible, then it won't be. I'm not saying to make a big leap from starting a new business to making one million dollars from it within a year. However, as you incrementally try new things and open yourself up to more possibilities, the more you will see the world change around you. Moving past any skepticism by trying and testing new things will help you determine what works for you and it will help you shift your beliefs. Remember from Part 3: The Mind that your beliefs create your reality.

Affordable & Accessible Self-Care

Self-care activities come in many forms, with some being more affordable and accessible than others. A lot of my favorite bodywork activities are free on YouTube (although that does require internet access). I find the most impactful self-care activities are absolutely free. Moving your body (i.e. stretching, going outside for a walk, body tapping, etc.) and taking a few minutes to take deep conscious breaths are some of the simplest, yet incredibly effective ways to change your state and connect within yourself. While it is great to get massages and have sports as hobbies (that likely require expensive equipment), it is truly not necessary in order to be able to access your mind-body connection. The most important thing is to practice accessing and strengthening your mind-body connection. The how of it doesn't matter as much as actually doing it.

Lack of Support Network

A support network is a great way to be held accountable to your goals as you practice unlocking your mind-body connection. If no one in your circle is supportive of these particular interests and goals of yours, then you may need to find a like-minded community for support in this area. Jim Rohn, author and entrepreneur, says, *"You are the average of the five people you spend the most time with."* While that feels like a strong statement, it's a great point to consider. The more time you spend with people that lift you up and support your goals, the more motivated you will be to continue your efforts. When you find yourself surrounded by people that are negative and don't want to see you succeed, you will have a harder time staying on track with your goals and making lasting change. It's not to say that it isn't possible, but it can definitely be more challenging.

I liken it to having snacks in the house and then trying not to eat them. If they are there, it is harder to resist the temptation. It's easier to not have the snacks in the house if you don't want to eat them. Then, there is no temptation to work against. While people aren't the same as snacks, it is helpful to keep in mind that the more supportive of an environment you have, the more potential you have to keep going and find success. If you don't have a supportive network right now, you can try joining some local or online communities to find people with similar interests. Also, since you're reading this book, you can consider me a friend. Please feel free to reach out on social media or my website. I am cheering you on!

If the people you live with aren't supportive of your growth efforts, continue to practice and strengthen your mind-body connection. The more you shift your inner world and hold your truth, the less of an impact the non-supportive people will have on your life until you're able to change your living situation.

Moving About The
World Differently

There really is a different way to move about this world if you allow yourself to believe it. As you become more aware of your own energy, your power, and your inner knowing, things will shift in your life. It might seem small at first . . . listening to your body to see if you're really hungry or not, if it's time to eat, and what you feel like having. Or perhaps it's regularly and intentionally incorporating brain breaks throughout your day, knowing that when you get back to work, you'll be refreshed and more productive. It might even be as simple as saying 5 things you are grateful for every day when you wake up and before you go to sleep.

All these small moments add up to something bigger. You begin to pave a new pathway and direction in your life. You'll question old beliefs and see the ways they are holding you back. Your thoughts will start to shift. As those thoughts shift, you begin to make different choices.

As I started applying this work to my day-to-day life, I decided I wanted to change my pattern of angry outbursts. Anytime I would have an angry outburst, I would allow it to take over my body and my mind. I'd scream and say mean things. Afterward, I would feel ashamed and embarrassed. What I realized is when you make this type of decision, it doesn't usually mean you flip a switch and then all of a sudden you don't have angry outbursts anymore. You need to reprogram your system. You need to learn new tools to work with. For example, learn how to identify your feelings and needs, communicate your needs, and live with less stress.

There will come a time where this new work takes a toll on you.

Perhaps your friends and family don't understand it, so you find you have fewer people to confide in. Or maybe you won't feel as motivated by your job and the work you do each day.

It may also feel tiring to always try to test your limits and make new choices. It is much easier to stay in our old patterns, even if we don't like the outcome. In the end, we may choose the familiar.

For me, this process has always felt like taking two steps forward and one step back. As long as you hold your intention and keep taking small steps, you will see the change in your daily life.

I find this work is neither easy nor hard. It simply is. There will be times and situations where you don't find it difficult to choose something different and make a change. Then there will be other times where you repeat the same pattern over and over and it feels incredibly hard to break through. Both are to be expected in any transformational journey. What I can tell you is that the more you tell yourself it will be easy, the more opportunities you have to learn your lessons with less resistance. That's what I've found to be true for myself with my experiences.

There is nothing I love more than working with clients to identify what works for them and guide them on their journey to creating the life they want to live. If you are looking for personalized support on your journey, you're invited to explore my offerings on my website, www.maryclavieres.com.

Part 6: Key Takeaways

Integration

- Integration is all about taking new information and incorporating it into your day-to-day life with new habits.

- If you slip up from your new habits, start again. Everyone falls from time to time. The real change comes from getting back up and trying again.

- The mind-body connection applies to life, home, and work. Pay attention to where you feel more connected or less connected.

- Celebrate your wins. The road to change can feel long and challenging. It's important to show up and celebrate yourself as a way to keep going.

- You are the creator of your life and your reality. Experiment and find what works best for YOU. Leave the rest behind.

Reminder:

Small steps add up to big impact.

Conclusion

I t is completely possible to have a life you love and to know yourself on deeper levels than you've ever known before. The first step is believing it. The second step is showing up and doing the work to get there.

The life you want to live is waiting for you. It is in the micro steps you take each and every day:

Every time you identify a negative thought and replace it with a positive one.

Every time you slow down and listen to what your body is telling you.

Every time you make a choice that is aligned with your soul calling.

Every time you take a step.

Every time you choose to keep going.

Every time you choose to show up.

Every time you allow yourself to create what you feel called to.

Every time you allow yourself to dream.

And every time you believe what you truly desire is possible for you.

All these pieces fall into place over time. All the small moments add up to something big. When you look back, you will see the small steps. You will see the times you moved in a straight line and the times you took the winding road. It all comes together in a unique path you created to be able to have the life you want. It's in the small moments. Over and over again.

Even though you may have big challenges—sometimes more than other times—this life is truly a gift. Your journey and your own potential expansion never stop being possible. Even if one day feels hard, you can pick yourself back up and start again. Dig deep and unlock your mind-body connection. Trust me, your life will never be the same again.

Reminder:

You are a miracle. Own this belief
as you walk this world.

Work With Mary

If you're ready to apply these concepts to what you're navigating in your life right now, whether it's a career change, business pivot, or life circumstance, I'd love to support you. You're invited to explore the following options:

Decision Making Accelerator Session

A personalized Decision Making Accelerator session is a powerful place to begin understanding how your mind-body connection and your unique energy work together. We'll explore how your energy is designed to flow, how you're uniquely wired to make decisions using your mind-body connection, and create an action plan for where to focus next.

1:1 Mentorship, Advisory & Coaching Containers

If you're navigating a career change or pivot in your business, seeking deeper alignment in your relationships, or feeling called to reconnect within yourself, I offer 1:1 mentorship containers tailored to your unique situation. In this supportive space, you'll be seen, guided, and held as you access the deeper layers of your inner wisdom. This is an invitation to strengthen your mind-body connection and move forward with grounded confidence and authentic presence.

Additional Resources

The *Find Yourself, Change Your Life* **podcast** – Tune into my weekly podcast where I explore topics related to the mind-body connection, personal transformation, Human Design, and living in alignment. Each episode offers insights, stories, and tools to support you on your journey toward a more connected and intentional life.

Mind-Body Connection Workbook – I wholeheartedly recommend downloading this workbook. Inside, you'll find resources, guided meditations, and reflective prompts designed to support you in deepening and nurturing your mind-body connection.

Thank you!

Thank you for taking the time to read *Mind-Body Connection Unlocked*. I hope you enjoyed the book and found it supportive to where you're are now. I encourage you to revisit parts of this book as you continue on your journey.

I would love if you could take a moment to leave a review on Amazon and / or Goodreads.

Scan this QR code to leave a review.

Acknowledgments

This book would not have been possible without the support of so many people.

Remy, Evie and Elena – I know I mentioned you all in the dedication, but you need to be on this list too. Thank you for choosing me, loving me, and encouraging me every single step of the way. I am so happy and proud of the life we've built. It is one of my life's greatest joys to spend my days with you.

Mom and Dad – thank you for your unwavering support and for believing in me every step of the way. From you, I have learned love, dedication, drive, perseverance, and creativity. You have shown me what it takes to run your own business while always reminding me to follow my dreams. Your stories and experiences have shaped me into who I am today, and I am deeply grateful.

Jennifer, Nick, and Christina – thank you for being by my side for basically my whole life (technically all of yours, haha). You continue to teach me about life and love in endless ways. I love you all so much.

Odile and Roland – Thank you for welcoming me in France with open arms and for celebrating all of my *French life* milestones with me. Also, thank you for always encouraging me with this book . . . even if Roland won't read it until it's translated into French.

Lionel, Melanie and Sylvain – thank you for being my extended siblings. I love you.

Cindy – without you, this book truly would not have been published . . . at least not anytime soon. Thank you for all of your support, encouragement, unwavering belief in me and for teaching me how to correctly format a manuscript. I'm so grateful to be on this journey with you.

Lara, Helen, Melissa, Amanda B., and Jamie L. – I'm so incredibly grateful our friendships have stayed strong, even if I'm across the ocean now. Thank you for your endless support, encouragement, and realness as we navigate life together.

Ashley – thank you for answering my endless questions about what it takes to structure, write, and birth a book into this world, all while juggling the ups and downs of life and parenting together.

Amanda F. – I truly don't know where I'd be without our conversations, your constant encouragement, and our crazy synchronicities. Thank you for all of it.

Hannah – I cherish our conversations about HD, parenting, life, business, and everything in between. Thank you for always encouraging me to live the fullest expression of my projector-ness.

Jamie P. – thank you for all of your incredible teachings on Human Design and for always encouraging me to think bigger.

Andrea – thank you for creating a space that witnesses and supports my healing as well as my growth and expansion. I deeply appreciate you.

Sarah and my Rebirth Sisters – I'm so happy to be pushing my edges every year in the beautiful circle of your unconditional love. I cherish and love you all so deeply.

Chelsea — my editor and publishing mastermind — thank you for all of your support in getting this book out into the world. I am so grateful to you for holding this book with your heart while I second guessed every single thing.

Thank you to each and every person who has supported me in some way. Whether you've liked or commented on a post, listened to a podcast episode, subscribed to my newsletter, or worked with me in some way—I am truly grateful for your presence.

And last, but certainly not least, thank you, dear reader, for picking up and reading this book. Your support means the world to me and without you, I wouldn't be able to do the work that I do. Thank you from the depths of my heart. May your ever-evolving journey continue to take you toward your highest alignment.

About The Author

Mary Clavieres is a transformation guide, mentor, and coach for those wanting to change their life in some way. Whether it is through life, relationships, or career, Mary's approach centers on the individual and meets them where they are to navigate change and transformation in a way that works best for them.

Mary has experienced many life changes that led her to this point in time. She believes that as each individual becomes more aligned with their truest nature, the world infinitely benefits.

When not speaking about the mind-body connection, human design, or coaching, Mary can be found in France, living with her husband and two daughters, walking in nature, reading, writing, and connecting with the beauty that is all around us.

NOTES

INTRODUCTION

1. "Regrets of the Dying," Bronnie Ware, https://bronnieware.com/blog/regrets-of-the-dying/

HOW TO USE THIS BOOK

1. "12 Famous Quotes That Always Get Misattributed," Christina Sterbenz, Business Insider, last modified Oct 7, 2013, https://www.businessinsider.com/misattributed-quotes-2013-10

THE SCIENCE OF THE MIND-BODY CONNECTION

1. "Studies on Mind/Body Connection," Intergris Health, https://integrishealth.org/resources/articles/studies-on-mind-body-connection
2. "Stress," World Health Organization, last modified February 21, 2023, https://www.who.int/news-room/questions-and-answers/item/stress
3. "How do emotions affect our body?", Dr. Lindsey, SLO Health Direct Primary Care, https://www.slohealthcenter.com/how-do-emotions-affect-our-body/
4. "Osteopath", Cambridge Dictionary, https://dictionary.cambridge.org/dictionary/english/osteopath
5. "Placebo", Oxford Languages Dictionary, https://www.oed.com/dictionary/placebo_n?tl=true
6. "The placebo effort: Amazing and real," Robert H. Shmerling, MD, Harvard Health Publishing, last modified June 22, 2020. https://www.health.harvard.edu/blog/the-placebo-effect-amazing-and-real-201511028544
7. "The power of the placebo effect," Howard E. LeWine, MD, last modified July, 22, 2024, https://www.health.harvard.edu/newsletter_article/the-power-of-the-placebo-effect

HEALING MODALITIES

1. "What is Cognitive Behavioral Therapy?", American Psychological Association, last modified 2017, https://www.apa.org/ptsd-guideline/patients-and-families/cognitive-behavioral
2. "Key Concepts of Cognitive Behavior Therapy (CBT)", Grouport, https://www.grouporttherapy.com/blog/cbt-key-concepts?5d78fb30_-

page=3#:~:text=The%20fundamental%20concepts%20of%20CBT,the%20va-lidity%20of%20automatic%20thoughts

3. "Sports stars who are committed to mental health," Sarina Scharpf, Listicle, last modified November 8, 2023, https://www.ispo.com/en/people/athletes-mental-health-issues

EMBRACING SELF-RESPONSBILITY

1. "Karpman drama triangle," Wikipedia, last modified May 25, 2025

5 PILLARS OF SELF-CARE

1. "8 Health Benefits of Sleep," Sleep Foundation, Jay Vera Summer, last modified February 29, 2024, https://www.sleepfoundation.org/how-sleep-works/benefits-of-sleep

2. "What Are Sleep Deprivation and Deficiency?" Sleep Deprivation and Deficiency, National Heart, Lung, and Blood Institute, last modified March 24, 2022, https://www.nhlbi.nih.gov/health/sleep-deprivation#:~:text=Sleep%20deficiency%20is%20 20linked%20to,adults%2C%20teens%2C%20and%20children.

3. "How many hours of sleep are good enough for health?" Adult Health, Mayo Clinic, last modified February 1, 2025, https://www.mayoclinic.org/healthy-lifestyle/adult-health/expert-answers/how-many-hours-of-sleep-are-enough/faq-20057898.

4. "Dehydration," Cleveland Clinic, last modified June 5, 2023, https://my.clevelandclinic.org/health/diseases/9013-dehydration

5. "Water: How much should you drink every day?" Nutrition and healthy eating, Mayo Clinic, last modified October 12, 2022, https://www.mayoclinic.org/healthy-lifestyle/nutrition-and-healthy-eating/in-depth/water/art-20044256#:~:text=About%2015.5%20cups%20

6. Mayo Clinic, "Water: How much should you drink every day?"

7. Cleveland Clinic. "Dehydration."

8. "What to Know About Seasonal Eating," WebMD Editorial Contributors, WebMD, last modified February 25, 2024, https://www.webmd.com/diet/what-to-know-seasonal-eating.

9. "Endorphins," Cleveland Clinic, last modified May 19, 2022, https://my.clevelandclinic.org/health/body/23040-endorphins.

10. "Why you should move — even just a little — throughout the day," Heart Health, Harvard Health Publishing, Harvard Medical School, last modified July 14, 2023, https://www.health.harvard.edu/heart-health/why-you-should-move-even-just-a-little-throughout-the-day.

11. "Alcohol," World Health Organization, last modified June 28, 2024, https://www.who.int/news-room/fact-sheets/detail/alcohol.

12. "What is Nicotine?" Nicotine Addiction, Addiction Center, last modified February 27, 2025, https://www.addictioncenter.com/nicotine/

ACTIVITY 2.4: IDENTIFY YOUR VALUES

1. "List of Values: 305 Value Words, Lists, PDFs, & Excel Sheets," Tchiki Davis, MA, PhD, Berkeley Well-Being Institute, accessed July 14, 2025, https://www.berkeleywellbeing.com/list-of-values.html

TOOL 2.1: JOURNALING

1. Cameron, Julia, *"The Artist's Way Morning Pages Journal: A Companion Volume to the Artist's Way,"* Tarcher, 1997.

TOOL 2.2: WALKS IN NATURE

1. "Nature and mental health," Mind, last modified April, 2025, https://www.mind.org.uk/information-support/tips-for-everyday-living/nature-and-mental-health/.

UNDERSTANDING THE MIND

1. "22 Facts About the Brain | World Brain Day," Julia Burke, Dent Neurologic Institute, accessed July 14, 2025, https://www.dentinstitute.com/22-facts-about-the-brain-world-brain-day/#:~:text=The%20average%20person%20has%20about%2012%2C000%20to%2060%2C000%20thoughts%20per%20day.)

MENTAL BLOCKS

1. "Imposter Syndrome," Merriam-Webster Dictionary, last modified July 4, 2025, https://www.merriam-webster.com/dictionary/imposter%20syndrome

CREATING A NEW REALITY

1. Oxford, English Dictionary, "Belief," last accessed on July 14th, 2025, https://www.oed.com/dictionary/belief_n?tab=factsheet#23828350
2. Oxford English Dictionary, "Thought," last accessed on July 14th, 2025, https://www.oed.com/dictionary/judgement_n?tab=factsheet#40220022
3. Oxford English Dictionary, "Perspective," last accessed July 14, 2025, https://www.oed.com/dictionary/perspective_v? tab=factsheet#13345273
4. Oxford English Dictionary, "Judgment," last accessed July 14, 2025, https://www.oed.com/dictionary/placebo_n?tl=true
5. Connors, Rogers, Smith, Tom, *Change the Culture, Change the Game: The Breakthrough Strategy for Energizing Your Organization and Creating Accountability for Results*, Portfolio Penguin, 2011.

THE ENERGY BODY

1. Alcantara, Margarita, *Chakra Healing: a Beginner's Guide to Self-Healing Techniques that Balance the Chakras,* Callisto Publishing, 2017.
2. "The Health Effects of Poor Sleep," Yale Medicine, last modified March 13, 2023, https://www.yalemedicine.org/news/effects-of-poor-sleep
3. "How to Make Better Decisions in Your Life & Business," Mary Clavieres, accessed July 14, 2025, https://www.maryclavieres.com/workshop

THE EMOTIONAL BODY

1. "What Is Box Breathing?", WebMD Editorial Contributor, last modified April 27, 2025, https://www.webmd.com/balance/what-is-box-breathing

A NEW WAY OF BEING

1. "What Is the Ego, and Why Does It Matter?" Charles A. Francis, Mindfulness Meditation Institute, last modified January 1, 2019, https://mindfulnessmeditationinstitute.org/2019/01/01/what-is-the-ego-and-why-does-it-matter/
2. "Ego as the Rational Part of Personality," Kendra Cherry, Very Well Mind, last modified October 31, 2023, https://www.verywellmind.com/what-is-the-ego-2795167.

TOOL 4.1: TAPPING

1. Lee, Ilchi, *Water Up Fire Down,* Best Life Media, 2020

BUILDING EMOTIONAL RESILIENCE & CONSISTENCY

1. "How Long Does it Actually Take to Form a New Habit? (Backed by Science)," James Clear, Behavioral Psychology, James Clear, accessed July 14, 2025, https://jamesclear.com/new-habit
2. "Time Spent Using Smartphones (2025 Statistics)," Fabio Duarte, Exploding Topics, last modified June 5, 2025, https://explodingtopics.com/blog/smartphone-usage-stats

PLANNING YOUR DAY—FINDING WHAT WORKS FOR YOU

1. "Average Human Attention Span Statistics & Facts [2024]," Samba Recovery, last modified March 4, 2025 https://www.sambarecovery.com/rehab-blog/average-human-attention-span-statistics

2. "Welcome to the Pomodoro® Technique," The Pomodoro® Technique, accessed July 14, 2025, https://www.pomodorotechnique.com/welcome/#

BIBLIOGRAPHY

Addiction Center. Nicotine Addiction. "What is Nicotine?" Last modified February 27, 2025. https://www.addictioncenter.com/nicotine/.

Alcantara, Margarita. *Chakra Healing: a Beginner's Guide to Self-Healing Techniques that Balance the Chakras.* Callisto Publishing. 2017.

American Psychological Association. "What is Cognitive Behavioral Therapy?" Last modified 2017. https://www.apa.org/ptsd-guideline/patients-and-families/cognitive-behavioral.

Burke, Julia. "22 Facts About the Brain | World Brain Day." Dent Neurologic Institute. Last accessed July 14, 2025. https://www.dentinstitute.com/22-facts-about-the-brain-world-brain-day/.

Cambridge Dictionary. "Osteopath." Last accessed July 14, 2025. https://dictionary.cambridge.org/dictionary/english/osteopath.

Cameron, Julia. *The Artist's Way Morning Pages Journal: A Companion Volume to the Artist's Way.* Tarcher. 1997.

Cherry, Kendra. Very Well Mind. "Ego as the Rational Part of Personality." Last modified October 31, 2023. https://www.verywellmind.com/what-is-the-ego-2795167.

Clavieres, Mary. "How to Make Better Decisions in Your Life & Business." Accessed July 14, 2025. https://www.maryclavieres.com/ workshop.

Clear, James. "How Long Does it Actually Take to Form a New Habit? (Backed by Science)." Behavioral Psychology. James Clear. Accessed July 14, 2025. https://jamesclear.com/new-habit.

Cleveland Clinic. "Dehydration." Last modified June 5, 2023. https://my.clevelandclinic.org/health/diseases/9013-dehydration.

Cleveland Clinic. "Endorphins." Last modified May 19, 2022. https://my.clevelandclinic.org/health/body/23040-endorphins.

Connors, Rogers, Smith, Tom. *Change the Culture. Change the Game: The Breakthrough Strategy for Energizing Your Organization and Creating Accountability for Results.* Portfolio Penguin. 2011.

Davis, Tchiki, MA, PhD. List of Values: 305 Value Words, Lists, PDFs, & Excel Sheets. Berkeley Well-Being Institute. https://www.berkeleywellbeing.com/list-of-values.html.

Dr. Lindsey. "How do emotions affect our body?" SLO Health Direct Primary Care. https://www.slohealthcenter.com/how-do-emotions- affect-our-body/.

Duarte, Fabio. "Time Spent Using Smartphones (2025 Statistics)." Exploding Topics. Last modified June 5, 2025. https://explodingtopics.com/blog/smart phone-usage-stats.

Francis, Charles. A. Mindfulness Meditation Institute. "What Is the Ego, and

Why Does It Matter?" Last modified January 1, 2019. https://mindful nessmeditationinstitute.org/2019/01/01/what-is-the-ego-and-why-does-it-matter/.

Grouport. "Key Concepts of Cognitive Behavior Therapy (CBT)."https://www.grouporttherapy.com/blog/cbt-key-concepts.

Harvard Health Publishing. Heart Health. "Why you should move — even just a little — throughout the day." Harvard Medical School. Last modified July 14, 2023. https://www.health.harvard.edu/heart-health/why-you-should-move-even-just-a-little-throughout-the-day.

Intergris Health. "Studies on Mind/Body Connection." Last accessed July 14, 2025. https://integrishealth.org/resources/articles/studies- on-mind-body-connection.

Karpman, Stephan B, MD. https://karpmandramatriangle.com/.

Lee, Ilchi. *Water Up Fire Down*. Best Life Media. 2020.

LeWine, Howard, E, MD. "The power of the placebo effect." Last modified July, 22, 2024, https://www.health.harvard.edu/ newsletter_article/the-power-of-the-placebo-effect.

L. Nummenmaa, E. Glerean, R. Hari, & J.K. Hietanen, Bodily maps of emotions, Proc. Natl. Acad. Sci. U.S.A. 111 (2) 646-651, https://doi.org/10.1073/pnas.1321664111 (2014).

Marks, Hedy. "What Is Holistic Medicine and How Does It Work?" Last modified November 16, 2023. https://www.webmd.com/balance/what-is-holistic-medicine.

Mayo Clinic. Adult Health. "How many hours of sleep are good enough for health?" Last modified February 1, 2025. https://www.mayoclinic.org/healthy-lifestyle/adult-health/expert-answers/how-many-hours-of-sleep-are-enough/faq-20057898.

Mayo Clinic. Nutrition and healthy eating. "Water: How much should you drink every day?" Last modified October 12, 2022. https://www.mayoclinic.org/healthy-lifestyle/nutrition-and-healthy-eating/in-depth/water/art-20044256.

Merriam-Webster Dictionary. "Imposter Syndrome". Last modified July 4, 2025. https://www.merriam-webster.com/dictionary/imposter%20syndrome.

Mind. "Nature and mental health." Last modified April, 2025. https://www.mind.org.uk/information-support/tips-for-everyday-living/nature-and-mental-health/.

National Heart, Lung, and Blood Institute. Sleep Deprivation and Deficiency. "What Are Sleep Deprivation and Deficiency?" Last modified March 24, 2022. https://www.nhlbi.nih.gov/health/sleep-deprivation.

Oxford English Dictionary. "Belief." Last accessed on July 14th, 2025. https://www.oed.com/dictionary/belief_n? tab=factsheet#23828350.

Oxford English Dictionary. "Judgment." Last accessed on July 14th, 2025. https://www.oed.com/dictionary/judgement_n? tab=factsheet#40220022.

Oxford English Dictionary. "Perspective." Last accessed July 14, 2025. https://www.oed.com/ dictionary/perspective_v? tab=factsheet#13345273.

Oxford English Dictionary. "Placebo." Last accessed July 14, 2025. https://www.oed.com/dictionary/placebo_n?tl=true.

Oxford English Dictionary. "Thought." Last accessed July 14, 2025. https://www.oed.com/dictionary/think_v2? tab=factsheet#18549255.

The Pomodoro® Technique. "Welcome to the Pomodoro® Technique." Last accessed July 14, 2025. https://www.pomodorotechnique.com/welcome/#.

Salmon, Maureen. "What is somatic therapy?" Harvard Health Publishing. Last modified July 7, 2023. https://www.health.harvard.edu/blog/what-is-somatic- therapy-202307072951.

Samba Recovery. "Average Human Attention Span Statistics & Facts [2024]." Last modified March 4, 2025. https://www.sambarecovery.com/rehab-blog/average-human-attention-span-statistics.

Scharpf, Sarina. "Sports stars who are committed to mental health." Listicle. Last modified November 8, 2023. https://www.ispo.com/ en/people/athletes-mental-health-issues.

Shmerling, Robert H, MD. "The placebo effort: Amazing and real." Harvard Health Publishing. Last modified June 22, 2020. https:// www.health.harvard.edu/blog/the-placebo-effect-amazing-and-real-201511028544.

Sterbenz, Christina. "12 Famous Quotes That Always Get Misattributed." Business Insider. Last modified Oct 7, 2013. https:// www.businessinsider.com/misattributed-quotes-2013-10.

Stoughton, Jason. "Scientists break through the wall of sleep to the untapped world of dreams." U.S. National Science Foundation. Last modified February 18, 2021. https://www.nsf.gov/science-matters/scientists-break-through-wall-sleep-untapped-world.

Summer, Jay Vera. "8 Health Benefits of Sleep." Sleep Foundation. Last modified February 29, 2024. https://www.sleepfoundation.org/ how-sleep-works/benefits-of-sleep.

Yale Medicine. "The Health Effects of Poor Sleep." Last modified March 13, 2023. https://www.yalemedicine.org/news/effects-of-poor-sleep.

Tchiki Davis, MA, PhD. "List of Values: 305 Value Words, Lists, PDFs, & Excel Sheets." Berkeley Well-Being Institute. Last accessed July 14, 2025. https:// www.berkeleywellbeing.com/list-of-values.html

Ware, Bronnie. "Regrets of the Dying." https://bronnieware.com/blog/regrets-of-the-dying/.

Ware, Bronnie. *The Top Five Regrets of the Dying: A Life Transformed by the Dearly Departing.* Hay House Inc, 2012.

WebMD Editorial Contributors. WebMD. "What Is Box Breathing?" Last modified April 27, 2025. https://www.webmd.com/balance/what-is-box-breathing.

WebMD Editorial Contributors. WebMD. "What to Know About Seasonal

Eating." Last modified February 25, 2024. https://www.webmd.com/diet/what-to-know-seasonal-eating.

Wikipedia. "Karpman drama triangle." Last modified May 25, 2025. https://en.wikipedia.org/wiki/Karpman_drama_triangle.

World Health Organization. "Alcohol." Last modified June 28, 2024. https://www.who.int/news-room/fact-sheets/detail/alcohol.

World Health Organization. "Stress." Last modified February 21, 2023. https://www.who.int/news-room/questions-and-answers/item/stress.